SEARCHING FOR SHARING

Searching For Sharing

Heritage and Multimedia in Africa

Edited by Daniela Merolla
and Mark Turin

https://www.openbookpublishers.com

All external links were active at the time of publication unless otherwise stated and have been archived via the Internet Archive Wayback Machine at https://archive.org/web

Digital material and resources associated with this volume are available at https://www.openbookpublishers.com/product/590#resources

World Oral Literature Series, vol. 7 | ISSN: 2050-7933 (Print); 2054-362X (Online)

ISBN Paperback: 978-1-78374-318-6
ISBN Hardback: 978-1-78374-319-3
ISBN Digital (PDF): 978-1-78374-320-9
ISBN Digital ebook (epub): 978-1-78374-321-6
ISBN Digital ebook (mobi): 978-1-78374-322-3
DOI: 10.11647/OBP.0111

Cover image: *Interview* (2008) by ICT4D.at, CC BY-SA 2.0. Image from Flickr, https://www.flickr.com/photos/ict4d/3068125986

All paper used by Open Book Publishers is SFI (Sustainable Forestry Initiative), PEFC (Programme for the Endorsement of Forest Certification Schemes) and Forest Stewardship Council(r)(FSC(r) certified.

Printed in the United Kingdom, United States, and Australia
by Lightning Source for Open Book Publishers (Cambridge, UK)

Contents

Notes on Contributors

Brahima Camara is Dean of the Faculty of Humanities, Languages and Linguistics (FLSL, Faculté des Lettres, des Langues et des Sciences du Langage) at the Université des Lettres et des Sciences Humaines de Bamako (ULSHB), Mali. He obtained a Ph.D. from the University of Bayreuth in 1998 with a study on Mande hunters' literature. Brahima also researches the *tirailleurs* and, more recently, the African riflemen who served in the French army. Email: brahimajabatenin@gmail.com

Graeme Counsel is a Lecturer in ethnomusicology for the Melbourne Conservatorium of Music at the University of Melbourne. His recent projects in West Africa include three Endangered Archives Programme awards for which he digitized and preserved the national sound archives of Guinea. Over 7,000 songs from the collection are available online at the British Library Sounds website. Email: counselg@unimelb.edu.au

Kofi Dorvlo is Senior Lecturer at the General and Liberal Studies Department of the University of Health and Allied Sciences in Ho, Ghana. He gained his undergraduate degree in English and Linguistics at the University of Ghana, and he did his graduate work at the same university, where he was appointed Research Fellow at the Language Centre. He was awarded a Ph.D. from Leiden University in 2008. His doctoral research, which was funded by the Endangered Languages Programme of the Netherlands Organization for Scientific Research (NWO), focused on the documentation of the language and culture of the Logba people. Email: gekd2000@yahoo.com

Jan Jansen obtained his Ph.D. from Leiden University in 1995 with a critical analysis of the oral sources of the Mali Empire. A French edition of his thesis was published in 2001 *Épopée-Histoire-Société – Le cas de Soundjata (Mali-Guinée)*. From 1996 to 1998 he was a postdoctoral researcher at Leiden University, and from 1999 to 2004 he was a Research Fellow of the Royal Netherlands Academy of Arts and Sciences (KNAW), based at Leiden. He then took up his present post as a Lecturer at the Institute of Cultural Anthropology at Leiden University, and since 2010 he has been the managing editor of *History in Africa – A Journal of Method*, published by Cambridge University Press. Email: JANSENJ@FSW.leidenuniv.nl

Russell H. Kaschula is Professor of African Language Studies and he holds the National Research Foundation (NRF) Chair in the Intellectualisation of African Languages, Multilingualism and Education hosted at Rhodes University, South Africa. Research pertaining to this Chair covers Applied Language Studies, Theoretical Linguistics and Literature. He obtained his Ph.D. in African Oral Poetry from Rhodes, a University to which he returned in 2006, having previously taught in the US. His most recent book, edited together with Ekkehard Wolff, is titled *Multilingual Education for Africa: Concepts and Practices* (2016). He also developed the literary term "technauriture" in order to create links between technology, aurality and literature. This research was published as a position paper by Cambridge University. His most recent literary work is a collection of short stories entitled *Displaced* (2013). One of his projects was a critique of the translation of *Alice in Wonderland* into nine African languages, which was published in the *Journal of African Cultural Studies* (2015), http://doi.org/10.1080/13696815.2016.1160827. Email: R.Kaschula@ru.ac.za

Daniela Merolla is Professor in Berber Literature and Art at the Institut National des Langues et Civilisations Orientales (INALCO), Sorbonne Paris-Cité, and member of the research group LACNAD (Langues et Cultures du Nord de l'Afrique et Diasporas). She taught and researched African Literatures and Media at Leiden University from 2003 to 2015. She obtained her Ph.D. in Comparative Literature with a dissertation on the interaction of oral and written genres in the construction of identity (Kabylia, Algeria) from Leiden University and the French "habilitation à diriger des recherches" with a work on the Berber/ Amazigh multilingual literary space from Aix-Marseille University. Her research focuses on African oral literary productions (Berber/Amazigh) as well as written literatures in African and European languages. Her publications include: *Multimedia Research and Documentation of Oral Genres in Africa – The Step Forward* (2012) (edited with J. Jansen and K. Naït-Zerrad); *Transcultural Modernities: Narrating Africa in Europe* (2009) (edited with E. Bekers and S. Helff); *De l'art de la narration tamazight (berbère)* (2006). Email: daniela.merolla@inalco.fr

Andriamanivohasina Rakotomalala is an ethnologist and filmmaker with a Ph.D. in Anthropology and Sociology. His research interests include the ethnology of everyday life, traditional rice farming, and the ancestors' daily worship in Imerina (Madagascar). His productions include: *Un siècle d'enseignement du malgache à Paris* (52 minutes), 2000; *Saisons du riz en Imerina* (52 minutes), 2004; *Le culte de Ranavalona à Anosimanjaka*, a trilogy (290 minutes), 2014; *IRCAM, Douze minutes de conversation avec son secrétaire général le professeur El Houssaïn El Moujahid, Rabat 21 avril 2015* (13 minutes), 2013. Email: dadobri@club-internet.fr

Brigitte Rasoloniaina is Senior Lecturer in Sociolinguistics of Africa and Madagascar (MCF/HDR) at the Institut National des Langues et Civilisations Orientales (INALCO), Sorbonne Paris-Cité, and a member of the research team PREFics (Plurilinguism, Representations, French Speaking Expressions, Informations, Communication, Sociolinguistic) at the University of Rennes 2. Her research is in the field of the urban linguistic landscape. Her publications include 'Le passeur de poésie traditionnelle ou à la reconquête du "verbe de ses morts"', in S. Meitinger, L. Ramarosoa, L. Ink, C. Riffard (eds), *Jean-Joseph Rabearivelo, Œuvres complètes, Tome 2. Le poète, le narrateur, le dramaturge, le critique, le passeur de langues, l'historien* (2012). Email: brigitte.rasoloniaina@inalco.fr

Jan Bender Shetler (Ph.D., University of Florida) is Professor of History at Goshen College. She conducted most of her field research in the Mara Region of Tanzania documenting oral tradition, and in the archives. Her work has explored the history of social memory, identity, environmental relations, and place from precolonial times to the present. Other research includes work in Harar, Ethiopia. She has edited a number of collections of locally written histories from the Mara Region, including *Telling Our Own Stories: Local Histories from South Mara, Tanzania* (2003), which was a finalist for the 2005 Paul Hair Prize (African Studies Association) and a Choice Outstanding Academic Title for 2003. She is currently working on a book manuscript, *A Gendered History of Social Network Memory in the Mara Region, Tanzania, 1880-Present*. Recent publications include an edited collection, *Gendering Ethnicity in African Women's Lives* (2015); a book *Imagining Serengeti: A History of Landscape Memory in Tanzania from Earliest Times to the Present* (2007), and numerous articles for diverse interdisciplinary journals and volumes. Email: jans@goshen.edu

Mark Turin is Associate Professor of Anthropology at the University of British Columbia, where he currently serves as Chair of the First Nations and Endangered Languages Program and as Acting Co-Director of the Institute for Critical Indigenous Studies. An anthropologist, linguist, and radio broadcaster, he has worked for twenty-five years in collaborative partnership with indigenous communities in the Himalayan region (Nepal, Bhutan, Sikkim, and cultural Tibet) and more recently in the Pacific Northwest of Canada. He is the author or co-author of four books, three travel guides, the editor of eight volumes, and the co-editor of the peer-reviewed Open Access journal *HIMALAYA*. Email: mark.turin@ubc.ca

Valentin Vydrin is Professor of Manding at INALCO, Paris, a researcher at Langage, Langues et Cultures d'Afrique Noire (LLACAN), and a senior member of the Institut Universitaire de France. He has a Ph.D. (with a study on the grammar of the Looma language) from St. Petersburg State University and a habilitation (with a study on the reconstruction of phonology and noun morphology of the Proto-Mande) from the same university. He is the author of numerous publications on the Bambara, Maninka, Looma, and Dan languages as well as on proto-Mande reconstruction and the corpora of the Manding languages. Email: valentin.vydrin@inalco.fr

Introduction

Daniela Merolla

The unbalanced accumulation of knowledge and material goods since the so-called European expansion[1] prompted contemporary African studies to reflect on concepts such as sharing, partnership, restitution, and (re)appropriation.[2] The chapters in this volume focus on the specific articulation of such notions when relating to research on oral literature. The researchers engage with multimedia documents that were initially produced within an academic context, challenging their abilities and willingness to think in terms of sharing their work with local communities, organizations, and storytellers. This sharing is significant, as these communities and storytellers were the scholars' partners in audio-visual research on African oral literatures. We refer to local communities and diasporas who speak the language of the studied genres of folktales, mythical and epic narratives, love poems, funeral lamentations, ritual incantations, urban songs and popular theater, among many others, whether the compositions are faithfully transmitted, renovated, changed, or newly created. The present volume also explores sharing as a method for constructing representative

1 The date of 1492 symbolically signals the starting point of the expansion of European empires and their colonisation of many peoples and regions in Africa, Asia, Australia, and New Zealand.

2 For example, see Africa-Europe Group for Interdisciplinary Studies (AEGIS) (2016) for the first aim of AEGIS, and the multiple references to strategic partnership in the Council for the Development of Social Science Research in Africa (CODESRIA) Strategic Plan in CODESRIA (2015). See also Hountondji (2009); Bates, Mudimbe and O'Barr (1993).

 https://doi.org/10.11647/OBP.0111.08

multimedia documents, whether the impetus lies with researchers, artists, or other cultural stakeholders.[3]

The experiences of "sharing" located in the scientific literature, including those presented in this volume, demonstrate a panorama that is both complex and experiencing rapid development. Sharing data and results among researchers, as well as between researchers and their various publics, is an active field of reflection and discussion. An example of this is the increasing phenomenon of open source publications that offer analyses and data that can be freely accessed.[4] In parallel, the issue of copyright — including a debate among the stakeholders of the documented verbal arts about how "rights" are distributed (or not distributed) among them — has become central to discussion of dissemination. For those who work with oral genres, this issue has developed to include an appreciation of "copy-debts", as Jan Jansen writes (2012). This is an idea intended to convey "the debt that the scholar owes to the community for the work that has been cooperatively produced" (quoted by Shelter in this volume: 33).

Sharing documents on "cultural heritage" with the concerned communities has taken a multimedia dimension since the 1960s. The idea of "shared anthropology" was advanced by the film director and ethnologist Jean Rouch who arranged projections of his films in the villages where he had made them. He also sometimes filmed at the request of documentary protagonists, taking their opinions into account. The reaction of the villagers to their images being included in the final product enriched the documentary by providing multiple

---

3 This volume derives from the project "Multimedia Research and Documentation of African Oral Genres: Connecting Diasporas and Local Audiences" funded by the Netherlands Organization for Scientific Research (NWO), Leiden University (NL), the University of Hamburg (Asia-Africa Institute), the University of Naples for Oriental Studies (IUO), the Institut National des Langues et Civilizations Orientales (INALCO) in Paris, the Centre of African Studies at the School of Oriental and African Studies (SOAS) in London, the World Oral Literature Project (Cambridge) and co-organized by the University of Bamako (Mali), the Language Centre of the University of Ghana (Accra, Ghana), and the School of Languages of Rhodes University (South Africa). We would like to thank all the colleagues involved and in particular Abdellah Bounfour (INALCO, Paris) and Khadija Mouhsine (University Mohammed V, Rabat) for their friendly cooperation in the organization of the final conference of the project in December 2013.

4 See, for example, "Dakar Declaration of Open Access" in CODESRIA (2015); "Debating Open Access" in British Academy for the Humanities and Social Sciences (2013); Hoorn and Graaf (2006).

perspectives. Nevertheless, such a practice is predicated on a unilateral decision by a film director who decides when and to whom to show the film and how to include people's reactions in the film's final version.[5] Though an innovative form of ethical restitution, "shared anthropology" still confirmed the power imbalance between the film maker and those being filmed.

The aspiration to "share" documented images was similarly expressed by David McDougall (2003 [1975]: 125) in his "participatory cinema", which, in the 1970s, called for opening up the process of filmmaking by taking the responses of its "subjects", i.e. the local participants, into consideration. McDougall argued that, in the end result, this process would improve documentaries:

> By giving them [the participants] access to the film, he [the filmmaker][6] makes possible the correction, addition, and illuminations that only their responses to the material can elicit. Through such an exchange a film can begin to reflect the ways in which its subjects perceive the world (McDougall 2003 [1975]: 125).[7]

A persuasive movement emerged in the 1990s when the notion of "repatriation" became diffused in the field of museums and archives. As indicated by Bell, Christen and Turin (2013), "repatriation" initially focused on the demand for restitution of hundreds of skeletons and bones that were, and sometimes still are, kept in anthropological museums worldwide. Native American, Australian, and African communities requested to have their ancestors' skeletal remains returned in order to celebrate funerals. Two strikingly painful African examples became known worldwide at the beginning of 2000. Sarah Baartman, a San woman, was repatriated and then buried at Hankey (South Africa) in 2002 after her cast and skeleton had been exposed at the Musée de L'Homme (Paris) until 1974. The so-called "El Negro", a San man, was buried in the Tsolofelo Park of Gaborone (Botswana) in 2000, after his

5 Lamarque (2016); Scheinman (2014); Stoller (1992: 170–173); Henley (2010: 310–336); Ruby (1991).

6 In the masculine form, as still used in the 1970s.

7 In "Beyond Observational Cinema", an article that was published in 1975 and reprinted in the 2003 version used here.

stuffed remains had been exposed in the Darder Museum of Banyoles (Spain) until the late 1990s.[8]

Over the past few years, the notion of repatriation has evolved to include a much broader project of restitution, sharing, and appropriation, which currently involves "digital return".[9] The latter term signifies the practice of giving digitalized copies of materials and documentation to local museums and to the communities, families, and individuals that are concerned. Again, this practice incites new questions and criticism concerning those who possess the institutional and individual power of retaining the "originals" and returning the digital "surrogates" (Bell, Christen and Turin 2013: 5, 8).

In the case of audio-video recordings of verbal art, it appears to be less appropriate to speak of the repatriation of "surrogates", as the copies are near-originals: they all give material form to the performance, or at least to its sounds and visual elements. Digitalization indeed offers a relatively simple way for the researchers to record performances, interviews, and other fieldwork moments, to share such recorded performances, and subsequently to return the digital copies to the concerned individuals by making them accessible online and/or in digital formats (CD-roms, DVDs, SDS cards etc.). In this case, however, other theoretical and ethical issues are encountered alongside many practical problems (see in this volume Shetler: 23 and Camara, Counsel and Jansen: 81). The issues lie not so much in the "original versus copy" conundrum (as in the case of human remains and material objects) but into what type of document the recorded performance is transformed into (see Camara, Counsel and Jansen, this volume: 81; Rasolonaina and Rakotomalala, this volume: 123) and then in the legal, social, and affective relationships that are created (see the contributions by Shetler: 23; Kaschula: 41; Dorvlo: 61; Vydrin: 109 in this volume).

8 Youé (2007). See also *Sara Baartman. Between Worlds. Voyagers to Britain 1700–1850*, Exhibition 8 March–17 June 2007, National Portrait Gallery at http://www.npg.org.uk/whatson/exhibitions/2007/between-worlds/exhibition-tour/baartman.php; Davies (2003); Gewald (2001); *Africa Resource* (2015). A link should be drawn between these two cases of brutal body/bones exposition and the racist categorization presenting the San "as the most wretched and degraded of all 'savages'" (Hudson 2004: 308). See also Fauvelle-Aymar (2002).

9 "Return" is considered a term less loaded with the sense of legal pursuits than "repatriation", see Shetler in this volume.

Bauman writes that audio recordings are able "to overcome the ephemerality of the human voice, to capture and fix an utterance [...] endowing it with the qualities of an object: autonomy, durability, and even materiality" (2011: 1). At the same time, audio-video recordings create "mirages" of performances because selection and (even when involuntary) manipulation are employed in whatever technique of recording is used, e.g. analogue or digital, audio, visual, or multimedia. As McDougall aptly writes: "The viewfinder [...] frames an image for preservation, thereby annihilating the surrounding multitude of images which could have been formed. [...] [The image] also becomes, through the denial of all other possible images, a reflection of thought" (2003 [1975]: 123). When a performance is materialized and made autonomous, durable, and object-like by framing and selecting it while capturing it on video, an "object" that can be "shared" or "returned" is created. However, what type of object is this? Do researchers create a reference model or a kind of literary standard from a snapshot? Do they create a "tradition" from the recorded oral genre that, when returned, will be transmitted and revitalized, excluding the versions and genres that are not recorded? Do they participate in the "heritagization" (a term we may derive from "patrimonalisation" in French) of performances becoming museum pieces or tourist objects more than living social interactions? Delving deeper into the issue of selection, do researchers need to collect all that is possible: are all songs and stories or each piece of music equally important/relevant? What is the role of random and non-predictable elements in audio-video recordings?

If participatory documentation of verbal arts — to paraphrase McDougall — offers a first solution, the narrative power inscribed in the editing control of the researcher still pervades the recordings (see discussion in Camara, Counsel and Jansen, this volume: 81). On the other hand, the editing control can also be "shared" by forms of partnerships and cooperation (see Shetler: 23 and Vydrin: 109), and the essays in this volume demonstrate how fruitful and innovative it is when local users, students, and artists decide to employ it in their own activities (see Kaschula: 41, Rasolonaina and Rakotomalala: 123). The crux of the issue is that the "object-like" performance of multimedia documentation is embedded in the knowledge which is constructed on/through such materials. As the chapters in this volume illustrate, multimedia documentation is inscribed with the research goals and approaches of the scholars who produce it, which again incites the question of what is being "shared". This issue clearly extends beyond audio-visual documentation, as illustrated in African studies through the classic example of the legacy of Marcel Griaule and his team's research on Dogon mythology. Griaule's scholarly legacy includes many published studies, archived fieldwork papers, collections of photos and objects, and documentary films, and has acquired substantial authority over time. Griaule created "the" authorized tradition of Dogon myths, which is now appropriated in Malian tourist circuits and cultural associations (Van Beek and Schmidt 2012; Jolly 2001–2002). Taking into account the controversy in the way fieldwork data was collected and interpreted (Van Beek 1991; Van Beek and Jansen 2000), it can be questioned what is and can be "returned" to Mali, to whom it can be returned, and by whom it can be returned:

> Bien que la tentation soit grande de les considérer comme des "enregistrements" et donc comme des témoignages objectifs, les données ainsi archivées ont été sélectionnées, organisées, retravaillés par M. Griaule et ses collègues en fonction de leurs présupposés théoriques, de leurs méthodes et de leurs objectifs de recherche. [...] Il ne faut donc pas se tromper d'objectif: ces archives ethnographiques — qui appartiennent aux ethnologues qui les ont produites — n'ont pas à être "rendues" au Mali, mais d'un point de vue scientifique, il serait souhaitable qu'elles soient davantage accessibles aux chercheurs maliens (Jolly 2001–2002: 24, 27).[10]

The notion of "reusability" can be beneficial in this aspect. The concept of reusability is developed from the perspective of evaluating "how to implement" both the opening of data and the results of the research by utilizing electronic databases. Barwick and Thieberger (2005: 141). write that the concept of reuse derives from the fields of ecology and

10 "Although the temptation is great to see them [the archived data] as 'records' and therefore as objective testimony, such archived data has been selected, organized, and reworked by Griaule and his colleagues according to their theoretical positions, their methods and their research objectives. [...] One must make no mistake about the aim: the ethnographic archives — belonging to ethnologists that produced them — do not have to be 'returned' to Mali but, from a scientific point of view, it would be strongly advisable that they are accessible to Malian researchers" [editor's translation].

computer programming (reduce, reuse, recycle), and that it invites researchers "to work with field recordings in a way that allows their further use as archival objects", i.e. objects that are thus available to multiple audiences.[11] Reusability refers primarily to a "technique" of organizing the recorded material. The first step is to provide metadata "since the ability to find and reuse video materials may depend a great deal on how the metadata and annotations associated with it are defined and structured" (Whyte 2009: 15). This would imply that the aim is to archive video material with maximum contextual information (see Dauphin-Tinturier 2012). The second step is the segmentation of videos and the cataloguing of the video fragments' content. This step is essential because it allows users to know what is recorded in different sequences. An initial step to sharing complex research multimedia documentation is, therefore, making it "reusable", with the metadata making the criteria of selection and interpretative framework as explicit as possible. Such a form of reusability, however, involves an enormous investment of time and effort, which is one of the constraints noted by the contributors to this volume and often observed by those working with the "return" of video materials.

Examining the legal, social, and affective relationships that audio-visual documentation create, competing interests between different "actors" emerge. An often-mentioned case concerns recordings that film activities reserved to specific groups, for example to only men, women or the elderly population. Community members wish to recover the right to make decisions regarding their cultural heritage and to grant access only to specific groups and individuals, while the researchers' universities, museums, and sometimes the researchers themselves often wish to ensure ongoing and wider data access, continuity, and maintenance of the collections.[12] The practice of meetings between

11 "Spoken words, embodied in ordinary speech, may be ephemeral physical processes. But they become things when they appear on paper, on artefacts or when they are recorded in magnetic or digital codes on tapes or disks, or in film or videotape" (Cruikshank 1992 in Laszlo 2006: 301).

12 Competing interests may also concern recordings of a sensitive nature because of their personal or political content. Compare on such issues the "Principles for Oral History and Best Practices for Oral History" of the Oral History Association adopted in 2009 and available at http://www.oralhistory.org/about/principles-and-practices and http://www.oralhistory.org/about/principles-and-practices/oral-history-evaluation-guidelines-revised-in-2000/#1.3.1

archivists, researchers, and the "representatives" of the community is certainly laudable, and it has provided beneficial results. A current "sharing" protocol is that the collected materials become accessible and reusable only by "authorized" groups and individuals in accordance with the local norms. In this manner, archivists, researchers, and community members hope to respect the idea that knowledge is widespread in a community, but not everyone knows everything.[13]

On the other hand, the question remains whether, by accepting such limits, social systems and groups are considered to be static. According to Schultz (1997: 457), men and women not belonging to the original families of "griots", a class of oral bards well-diffused in Western Africa, could "democratize" the previous monopoly over knowledge, history, and the legitimization of power by learning from cassettes and radio. In such a case, technology allows the "new" griots to go beyond the rigid social divides of knowledge. Authorization to access recordings following restrictions based on age, sex, and social group may thus no longer meet the expectations of, for example, young people and women who do not accept being excluded from certain rituals and forms of knowledge. The concept of representatives in the "authorization system" is similarly at stake. As indicated by Shetler in this volume (23), scholars and archivists are usually in contact with so-called community gatekeepers "without questioning the dynamics behind their authority" (35). However, researchers must ask: who represents whom? Do the members of the (men's) assembly represent all the village? Do the representatives of political parties or the members of ritual societies or cultural or economic organizations represent it as well? It is likely that there will always be someone who is not represented.

A second issue concerns how groups and individuals within the community perceive the oral genres, and what they want of them. Do all community members appreciate and desire the researcher's documentation of oral performances? This question is not rhetorical. In this volume, Rasoloniaina and Rakotomalala (123) cite Glowczewski (2005: 14) asserting that what people demand "back" is "the right to talk with authority on the knowledge that is theirs" and not the recordings of verbal arts. An explicit case in point is offered by the scholar

13 On unevenly distributed cognition and knowledge, see Romney, Weller and Batchelder (1987).

Mingzong Ha, who reported the skeptical reaction of a young man during a project to record family histories of migration of the Mongghul Ha Clan (China). While members of the older generation considered it important to have their words and memories recorded, the young man was dubious about the project because this type of information and documentation "did not enhance skills learnt at school and was not helpful in finding employment" (Mingzong, Mingzhu and Stuart 2013: 146). Another intriguing example is provided by Volume 4 of the *Verba Africana Series* which explores whether multimedia documentation of oral genres should take into account that the "sharing" of research recordings online can sustain individuals' and sub-groups' myth-making for specific political and religious purposes (Merolla, Ameka and Dorvlo 2010).

As "sharing" linked to participation is fruitful, one can advocate integrating the research on verbal arts with interviews and questionnaires to determine what results, documents, and "discourse" are interesting for various members and groups of the community and to what ends they are significant. Interviews and questionnaires, for example, could be addressed to those who are employed in primary and secondary schools and their pupils, to university students and teachers, to cultural and economic organizations, to elders and other members of rural communities, and to individual storytellers and poets. Once again, a huge investment of time and work is required in such a form of "sharing" which, therefore, might prove to be difficult in practice.

In conclusion, the concepts of sharing, repatriation, return, restitution, and reusability refer to groups and individuals retaining physical/verbal materials and knowledge that were shared (voluntarily or not) with the researchers and that are made accessible once again to the first stakeholders.[14] At the same time, all of these terms convey the sense that the researchers hold possession of the object-like "product", i.e. the scientific knowledge produced by their intellectual efforts — often constituted in dialogue with the cultural stakeholders — including but also extending beyond the materials/documentation/knowledge on which it is based. Repatriation, restitution, and return, focusing

14 "The nomenclature of 'return' more honestly names the power and ultimate ownership in the transaction" (Geismar 2013: 257 cited by Shetler in this volume: 25).

on the former aspect, make explicit the legal and ethical imperative to return what was taken away. Sharing, as a concept, is less explicit about the power imbalance between who is giving and who is taking, but takes into account the research/scientific knowledge developed on/from the documentation. In this sense, we could think of using "partnership" — the term utilized by the Council for the Development of Social Science Research in Africa (CODESRIA) — and "reusability" as seen above, to include all users as stakeholders whether they are members of communities, researchers, institutional actors, or various online and offline publics. Whatever terms one decides to use, they refer not only to physical/verbal materials but also to the knowledge constructed on or by such materials, which complicates and blurs the terms of the exchange.

Do the issues mentioned above indicate that it would be best to dismiss the enterprise of partaking in verbal arts research documentation altogether? The chapters included in this volume demonstrate that this is not the case. The contributions of Shetler (23) and Camara, Counsel and Jansen (81) discuss at length and offer (some) answers to the questions of representativeness, "authorization", and copyright, while the chapters by Kaschula (41), Dorvlo (61) and Rasoloniaina and Rakotomalala (123) address how local intellectuals and artists re-use research and documentation of oral genres in educational environments.

In the first chapter, "The Mara Cultural Heritage Digital Library: The Implications of the Digital Return of Oral Tradition" (23), Jan Bender Shetler reflects on her digital library that acts as a repository for recordings and research regarding oral tradition and historical memory in the Mara Region (Tanzania). This digital library responds to the researcher's desire to "share", as well as to the desire of her network in the Mara Region to hear the recordings of their grandparents and elders who had been interviewed since the mid-1990s. Shetler initially examines both the pros and cons of sharing research in a book format, through multimedia, and online. Technical decisions play a role in relationship to the "ethical and political dilemmas" as online facilities should allow community members to make decisions about Open Access, access by request, or other forms of protocols. However, the core issue concerns who has "rights" to the documentation, who is entitled to access what information, and how they are able to do so.

Shetler very aptly traces the international debate on copyrights and clarifies how the reflection on ownership led her to implement a "fair-use" agreement, envisaging a release of copyrights from the scholar to the community. The intention was to provide community members the rights and control over the library, and to provide interested individuals (youth and local/international scholars) the opportunity to contribute to it. An important point is that the recordings are in local languages, a fact that "naturally limits who can use it and makes it an important source of material for language preservation" (34). Whatever interest the digital library will incite in the Mara region, Shetler sensibly concludes that preservation and vitality of the culture is, and remains in, the hands of the community itself.

Russell Kaschula's chapter, "Technauriture as a Platform to Create an Inclusive Environment for the Sharing of Research" (41), focuses on the specific case of South African oral literature research that "has fed back into the community from an educational perspective". The chapter first discusses "technauriture" as the conceptualization of verbal arts in the context of a technologized world and subsequently presents three case studies that are part of educational projects in isiXhosa. Such projects include the participation of local researchers and of community members as research assistants and interpreters to assist non-local students/academics. They recorded an extensive number of interviews, conversations, storytelling, and traditional court cases as well as diviners' songs, village choirs, women's traditional songs, initiation songs, and children's games in, respectively, the Mankosi area and the town of Keiskammahoek (Eastern Cape Province of South Africa). The research output consists of recordings of performances and a written translation, as well as videos of the interviewers/researchers watching, listening to, and translating the recordings into English. Recordings, videos, and translations were analyzed by students and academics and disseminated back in digital form to the community, in part due to the facilities offered by the International Library for African Music (ILAM). Another project discussed in the chapter is the Broster Beadwork Collection, which includes the narratives and songs linked to beadwork. This utilizes postgraduate students "to further document the beadwork, the role of beadwork in society and the societal value of the specific beads at hand" (56). The chapter concludes by suggesting that participatory research and digital return as well as endorsing novel links between research and the various partners (external researchers and community researchers) could feasibly have a circular effect on the technologizing of performances, i.e. the "technauriture" in them.

In the chapter "From Restitution to Redistribution of Ewe Heritage: Challenges and Prospects" (61), Kofi Dorvlo introduces the readers to the complexity of the Hogbetsotso, a yearly festival that has been celebrated in the Ewe area of Southern-eastern Ghana since the Anlo Ewe instituted it in the early 1960s. The celebrations aim at physically and spiritually cleansing the community. Rituals also support reconciliation among all community members as well as among community leaders such as the *Awomefia* (the King of Anlo), his military and administrative officers, the Field Marshall, and the Chiefs of the Right, Left, and Central wings. A central moment of the festival is the re-enactment of the migration stories narrating the journey of the Ewes from present-day Benin to present-day Ghana and Togo where they settled in the early seventeenth century after various displacements and subdivisions. Dorvlo explains that there is a growing "industry" of recording and selling rituals, including the Hogbetsotso, by local/national radios, TVs, video agencies, and cameramen, and that many videos are also available on social media. A significant number of recordings, nevertheless, is not sufficient for safeguarding cultural heritage. Fieldwork shows that in Anloga, the capital of the Anlo Ewe, the common knowledge on the organization and various meanings of the celebration is simplistic and influenced by the oppositional attitude of the Christian charismatic faith. The chapter concludes with the suggestion of pressuring the authorities to place topics on the Hogbetsotso and other rituals in the school curriculum, to introduce a heritage week, and to archive the research results and materials in local museums. This would allow preservation and sharing, as well as making the materials "relevant and beneficial to the Anlo State and the Ewe people in a globalized world with competing cultural contacts and influences" (62).

Brahima Camara, Graeme Counsel and Jan Jansen reflect on video research and the use of social media for educational aims in "YouTube in Academic Teaching: A Multimedia Documentation of Siramori Diabaté's Song 'Nanyuman'" (81). This contribution unveils the "backstage" of the research, informing the readers on all of the steps, starting from Graeme Counsel contacting Jan Jansen, who then contacted Brahima Camara, to develop a multimedia teaching tool: a YouTube video with accompanying text of the great Malian singer Siramori's hit "Nanyuman". The chapter discusses two main ethical/legal problems. The first one concerns the informal acquisition process of the copy of the video during Counsel's archival research at the Radio Télévision Guinée (RTG), and the researcher's decision about his "moral community". The second one involves the intricate issue of copyrights, as indicated by Shetler in this volume (23), which is further complicated by the accessibility through YouTube. The three authors write that they were unable to determine whether the copyrights are owned by "the performer, her inheritors, the griots of Kela [where Siramori grew up and received her artistic training], the ORTM, YouTube, or a combination of these stakeholders" (86). The impossibility to establish ownership and a representative community in a context where rights are "multi-layered and often situational", as well as the documentary importance of the video led the three scholars to make the decision to share the product of their research. However, they remain cognizant that this form of sharing offers documentary reputation and memory, but does not bring local artists economic profit.

The question as to whether groups and individuals within the community are interested in a researcher's documentation emerges from Valentin Vydrin's contribution "New Electronic Resources for Texts in Manding Languages" (109). Vydrin collected a huge amount of books and booklets in Manding languages, which are now digitized and available online through the "Bambara Electronic Library" and the "Bambara Reference Corpus", together with materials made available by the Académie Malienne des Langues and other Malian and international researchers. The idea is to have a substantial amount of open source "written documentation" for both researchers and the interested public, whether the texts are published in limited local editions, out of print, or belong to international series. Valentin Vydrin and his collaborators also hope to sustain the circulation of literacy in Manding languages, which are often considered as being only "oral languages" by the speakers and their environment in Mali and Guinea. Although the documentation collected by Vydrin is written and does not include audio-visual materials at the moment, it is highly relevant. It shows that the local interest varies among classes of individuals: the writing in Nko has a much broader appeal, while literacy in Bambara, written in the Latin alphabet, seems to remain limited to the intellectual elite and the urban middle class.

The volume concludes with the reflection on the "return" of oral literature research in Madagascar. In "Questioning 'Restitution': Oral Literature in Madagascar" (123), Brigitte Rasoloniaina and Andriamanivohasina Rakotomalala present three generations of local intellectuals, colonial researchers and missionaries, showing that the numerous transcriptions of oral genres in Malagasy constitute one viable form of restitution. Under the reign of King Ramana I in the 1820s, the Latin script was introduced alongside a rapid literacy campaign, leading to the constitution of local intellectuals who began to collect oral tales. The impetus provided to the collection of oral literature and book publishing in the Malagasy language, with and without translation in English and French, continued during the colonial period. The "return" is effected, in this case, by the written-oral circulation of the tales. The first example introduced is European tales translated into Malagasy, which, widely used in schoolbooks together with local stories, were already known orally among illiterates at the end of the nineteenth century. Other examples include Malagasy tales and myths circulating widely as modified plots or motifs within textbooks. Conversely, the "return" of contemporary video recordings and documentaries, which may be believed as more viable in an oral context, is much less effective. Documentaries attract national and international attention, but are hardly known in the countryside because of the serious restriction of facilities such as cinemas/theaters and the internet. The Malagasy case exhibits the pivotal role played by local intellectuals and "traditionalists" who take documentation, diffusion, and restitution into their own hands, and maintain that their production "must also be part of an exchange where the 'indigenous' (in the words of the old folklorists) aren't subsumed into an interpretative work, but become actors in this work" (138).

The contributions of this volume aptly explore the idea of sharing oral genres, and of "partnering" to enter into dialogue about the cultural stakeholders' expectations and about what they can produce and offer through new media.

References

AEGIS (2016) "Share Intellectual Resources", http://www.aegis-eu.org/why-aegis

Africa Resource (2015) "African Reburied after 170 Years in Spanish Museum", http://www.africaresource.com/essays-a-reviews/race-watch/69-african-reburied-after-170-years-in-spanish-museum

Baartman, Sara (2007) *Between Worlds. Voyagers to Britain 1700–1850*, Exhibition 8 March–17 June, National Portrait Gallery, http://www.npg.org.uk/whatson/exhibitions/2007/between-worlds/exhibition-tour/baartman.php

Barwick, L., and Thieberger, N. (2005) "Cybraries in Paradise: New Technologies and Ethnographic Repositories", in: Kapitzke C. and Bruce B. C. (eds.) *New Libraries and Knowledge Spaces: Critical Perspectives on Information and Education* (Mahwah NJ, Lawrence Erlbaum Associates): 133–149.

Bates, R. H., Mudimbe V. Y. and O'Barr J. F. (eds.) (1993) *Africa and the Disciplines: The Contributions of Research in Africa to the Social Sciences and Humanities* (Chicago, University of Chicago Press).

Baumam, R. (2011) "'Better than any Monument': Envisioning Museums of the Spoken Word", *Museum Anthropology Review* 5–1/2: 1–13.

Bell, J. A., Christen K. and Turin M. (2012) "Introduction: After the Return (Digital Repatriation and the Circulation of Indigenous Knowledge)", *Museum Anthropology Review* 7–1/2: 1–21.

British Academy for the Humanities and Social Sciences (2013) "Debating Open Aom", http://www.britac.ac.uk/openaccess/debatingopenaccess.cfm

CODESRIA (2016) "Strategic Plan", http://www.codesria.org/spip.php?article438&lang=en

— (2016) "Dakar Declaration of Open Access", http://www.eifl.net/news/dakar-declaration-open-access

Cruikshank, J. (1992) "Oral Tradition and Material Culture: Multiply Meanings of 'Words' and 'Things'", *Anthropology Today* 8–3: 5–9.

Dauphin-Tinturier, A.-M. (2012) "Performance, Hypermédia, et Propriété Intellectuelle", in: Merolla, D., Jansen, J. and Naït-Zerrad, K. (eds.) *Multimedia Research and Documentation of Oral Genres in Africa: The Step Forward* (Zurich/Berlin, Lit Verlag): 48–62.

Davies, C. (2003) *The Return of El Negro* (Johannesburg, Penguin Books).

Fauvelle-Aymar, F.-X. (2002) *L'Invention du Hottentot. Histoire du regard occidental sur les Khoisan, XVe-XIXe siècle* (Paris, Publications de la Sorbonne).

Geismar, H. (2013) "Defining the Digital", *Museum Anthropology Review* 7–1/2: 254–263.

Gewald, J. B. (2001) "El Negro, el Niño, Witchcraft and the Absence of Rain in Botswana", *African Affairs* 401: 555–580.

Glowczewski, B. (2005) "Lines and Criss-Crossings: Hyperlinks in Australian Indigenous Narratives", *MIA (Media International Australia) Digital Anthropology* 116: 24–35.

Henley, P. (2010) *The Adventure of the Real: Jean Rouch and the Craft of Ethnographic Cinema* (Chicago/London: University of Chicago Press).

Hoorn, E. and Graaf, M. (2006) "Copyright Issues in Open Access Research Journals: The Authors Perspective" *D-Lib Magazine* 12–2, http://www.dlib.org/dlib/february06/vandergraaf/02vandergraaf.html

Hountondji, P. J. (2009) "Knowledge of Africa, Knowledge by Africans: Two Perspectives on African Studies", *RCCS Annual Review* 1–1, https://rccsar.revues.org/174

Hudson, N. (2004) "'Hottentots' and the Evolution of European Racism", *Journal of European Studies* 34–4: 308–332.

Jansen, J. (2012) "'Copy Debts'? — Towards a Cultural Model for Researchers' Accountability in an Age of Web Democracy", *Oral Tradition* 27–2: 351–362.

Jolly, E. (2008) "Le fonds Marcel-Griaule: un objet de recherche à partager ou un patrimoine à restituer?", *Ateliers du LESC* 32, http://ateliers.revues.org/2902

Lamarque, P. (2016) *Le roi ne meurt jamais: le retour au "Roi". Feedback du film ethnographique et partage de l'anthropologie*, http://antoine.chech.free.fr/textes-colloque-JR/Lamarque.pdf

Laszlo, K. (2006) "Ethnographic Archival Records and Cultural Property", *Archivaria* 61: 300–307.

McDougall, D. (2003 [1975]) "Beyond Observational Cinema", in: Hockings, P. (ed.) *Principles of Visual Anthropology* (Berlin, Mouton de Gruyter): 115–132.

Merolla, D. Ameka, F. And Dorvlo, K. (2010) "Hogbetsotso: Celebration and Songs of the Ewe Migration Story. Interview with Dr. Datey-Kumodzie", in: *Verba Africana Series*, vol. 4 (Leiden, Leiden University), http://www.hum2.leidenuniv.nl/verba-africana/hogbetsotso

Mingzong, Ha, Mingzhu Ha and Stuart, C. K. (2013) "Mongghul Ha Clan Oral History Documentation", in: Turin, M., Wheeler, C. and Wilkinson, E. (eds.) *Oral Literature in the Digital Age. Archiving Orality and Connecting with Communities* (Cambridge, Open Book Publishers): 133–158, http://dx.doi.org/10.11647/OBP.0032

Oral History Association (2009) "Principles for Oral History and Best Practices for Oral History", http://www.oralhistory.org/about/principles-and-practices and http://www.oralhistory.org/about/principles-and-practices/oral-history-evaluation-guidelines-revised-in-2000/#1.3.1

Romney, A. K., Weller, S. and Batchelder, W. H. (1987) "Culture as Consensus: A Theory of Culture and Informant Accuracy", *American Anthropologist* 8–2: 313–338.

Ruby, J. (1991) "Speaking for, Speaking about, Speaking with, or Speaking alongside: an Anthropological and Documentary Dilemma", *Visual Anthropology* 7–2: 50–67.

Scheinman, D. (2014) "The 'Dialogic Imagination' of Jean Rouch: Covert Conversations in Les Maîtres Fous", in: Grant, B. K. and Sloniowski, J. (eds.) *Documenting the Documentary: Close Readings of Documentary Film and Video. New and Expanded Version* (Detroit, Wayne State University Press): 178–195.

Schultz, D. (1997) "Praise without Enchantment: Griot, Broadcast Media, and the Politics of Tradition in Mali", *Africa Today* 44–4: 443–464.

Stoller, P. (1992) *The Cinematic Griot: The Ethnography of Jean Rouch* (Chicago/London, University of Chicago Press).

Van Beek, W. E. A. (1991) "Dogon Restudied: A Field Evaluation of the Work of Marcel Griaule", *Current Anthropology* 32–2: 139–167.

Van Beek, W. E. A. and Jansen, J. (2000) "La mission Griaule à Kangaba (Mali)", *Cahiers d'Études Africaines* 158: 363–376.

Van Beek, W. E. A. and Schmidt, A. (eds.) (2012) *African Hosts and their Guests: Dynamics of Cultural Tourism in Africa* (Oxford, James Currey).

Whyte, A. (2009) "Roles and Reusability of Video Data in Social Studies of Interaction", *SCARP Case Study No. 5, Digital Curation Centre, Project Report 19 October 2009,* http://www.dcc.ac.uk/scarp

Youé, C. (2007) "Sara Baartman: Inspection/Dissection/Resurrection", *Canadian Journal of African Studies/Revue Canadienne des Études Africaines* 41–3: 559–567.

1. The Mara Cultural Heritage Digital Library: The Implications of the Digital Return of Oral Tradition

Jan Bender Shetler

Introduction[1]

The ethical issues around repatriation of African artifacts have long been at the center of practice for archeologists and museum specialists who continue to struggle with whether material artifacts should be taken out of their country of origin or not, and in either case how they can be protected and displayed over the long term. They have confronted the issues of where the necessary resources come from for protecting and curating these artifacts in a museum. Considerable work on ownership and display of cultural heritage has come out of conflicts in the US and Canada over the intellectual property rights of Native Americans, resulting in the Native American Graves Protection and Repatriation Act (NAGPRA 1990) as well as the National Museum of the American Indian Act (NMAIA 1989) in the US, and the First Peoples' Heritage, Language and Culture Act (1990) in British Columbia, Canada. The mandate from this work is that indigenous peoples must have a say and

1 This chapter was originally presented at the Annual Conference of the African Studies Association, Baltimore, 22 November 2013.

 https://doi.org/10.11647/OBP.0111.01

some control over how they are represented and who gets to use their cultural symbols (Brown 2003; Lonetree 2012; Mihesua 2000). Outside of North America, the same issues of legal rights were enshrined by UNESCO's program for Masterpieces of Oral Intangible Heritage of Humanity. The ethical and responsible actions of scholars in regard to the return of cultural materials now became no longer a choice but a matter of both social justice and law.

Those of us who work with oral tradition or oral history in Africa have only belatedly begun to face up to these issues. While oral historians have long used depositories like the Archives of Traditional Music at Indiana University, one might note the similarity to collections of antiquities from all over the world in the British Museum — preserved but largely inaccessible to the people whose ancestors produced them.[2] This becomes then an ethical as well as a technological issue. Even if we are convinced of the ethical obligation to repatriate this material, there remains substantial questions of how that would happen and how it would be received. I am grateful to the many scholars who have worked to develop this as a field of scholarship and practice, particularly having benefitted from the discussions around the 2012 workshop "After the Return: Digital Repatriation and the Circulation of Indigenous Knowledge", published in 2013 in the *Museum Anthropology Review*.

New digital technologies have made access to cultural materials possible in ways not previously imagined. Large scale projects like the World Digital Library, operated by both the US Library of Congress and UNESCO, are making digital website collections of primary documents and cultural treasures freely available and accessible around the world.[3] Other collections include oral material in conjunction with partner communities, such as what is featured on the Digital Return website, the Digital Himalaya Project, and The Smithsonian Recovering Voices Initiative or the World Oral Literature Project, among others.[4] The

2 Archives of Traditional Music, Indiana University, Bloomington, "Mission", http://www.indiana.edu/~libarchm/index.php/about-us.html

3 "About the World Digital Library", http://www.wdl.org/en/about

4 Digital Return, http://digitalreturn.wsu.edu; The Digital Himalaya Project, http://www.digitalhimalaya.com; The World Oral Literature Project http://www.oralliterature.org; The Smithsonian Recovering Voices Initiative http://recoveringvoices.si.edu

First Peoples' Cultural Council Collaboration works with communities in Canada, the US, and Australia to collect and digitally archive indigenous language materials.[5] Other groups digitally presenting African oral material include the Sierra Leone Heritage Project and the Africa On-line Digital Library.[6]

Many scholars working alongside community partners within museums prefer the term "digital return" over "repatriation" of cultural artifacts to indicate a less law-oriented and more relationship-oriented process of community stewardship (Bell, Christen and Turin 2013 — also see this article for a discussion on the significance of NAGPRA legislation). Hennessey *et al.* (2013: 45) describe digital return as "a process of creating and maintaining relationships between heritage and cultural institutions, people, and digital data". Within this emerging paradigm, museums make digital copies of artifacts and return only the digital version to the community. The nomenclature of "return" more honestly names the power and ultimate ownership in the transaction (Geismar 2013: 257). Projects in community-based participatory research are pushing the concept one step further by seeking not only to archive but produce materials in conjunction with the people who claim it as their heritage (cf. Atalay 2012; Robertson 2012). The issues of digital return are particularly acute in places of the world like Africa, which suffer from the inequities of computer infrastructure access and quality, but who are also jumping over the digital divide in terms of cell phone access (Geismar 2013: 254–263).

My own historical research in oral tradition has been in the Mara Region of Tanzania over the past twenty years. I am now working to digitally return these primary sources to the communities that produced them, however ambiguous that may be in reality. The example of the Mara Cultural Heritage Digital Library demonstrates the obstacles to completing that goal but also reiterates that returning this material in digital form involves a process of ongoing community dialogue and, above all, building long-term relationships.

5 First Peoples' Cultural Council, http://www.fpcc.ca

6 The Africa Online Digital Library, http://www.aodl.org; The Sierra Leone Heritage Project http://www.sierraleoneheritage.org

The Digital Return of Research in Oral Tradition

Since 1995, I have been interviewing elders, both men and women, in at least thirteen different language and ethnic groups of the Mara Region about oral tradition and historical memory. This region is particularly diverse, encompassing Southern Nilotic Tatoga, Eastern Nilotic Maasai, and Western Nilotic Luo as well as a great variety of East Nyanza Bantu languages including Kuria, Jita, Ikoma, and Ngoreme to name only a few. It remains one of the poorest, most isolated, and least studied areas in the nation, only recently discovered as a western portal to the Serengeti National Park along the park's corridor to Lake Victoria. The materials I have collected include hundreds of audio and video files, music, transcripts, photos, maps, and more. In the process of my research and my previous work in the region as a development worker, I have generated a large network of relationships with community elders, churches, and government officers, and have been adopted into a family that helped to facilitate my research. This is the basis on which "return" will be negotiated.

Hardcopy publications of my research material have been largely inaccessible in Tanzania, even when published in-country and in local languages. My publications of books and articles in US academic presses, including *Imagining Serengeti: A History of Landscape Memory in Tanzania from Earliest Times to the Present* (Shetler 2007), seek to interpret this region to students and scholars of African history. But I have also worked hard to make sure that some of the material that my local partners wanted to see in print was also published. I edited two collections, *Telling our own Stories* (Shetler 2003) and *Grasp the Shield Firmly, the Journey is Hard* (Shetler 2010) that took writing by elders themselves about their own oral traditions and published them in both Europe, and the US, as well as in Tanzania. These projects emerged as elders contacted me to see if I could help them publish the oral traditions they had documented. In both collections, the texts have facing pages in Swahili (or Luo) and English so that local people, as well as outsiders, could read the material. But the state of the publishing business in Dar es Salaam is in such dire straits that the publisher is reluctant to print too many copies of the books, fearing that they will sit unsold in boxes, and the press does not have money to commit to marketing or shipping copies around the country. Therefore, people in the rural Mara Region, far removed from Dar es Salaam, still have little-to-no-access to these books, which might as well be published in the US. In fact, one of these books is available in Print-on-Demand in the US and Europe through Amazon but is almost impossible to get in Tanzania. People in the Mara Region delight in getting these books when I give them away, but when they are available in local bookstores the price is prohibitive. Although barely enough to just cover the printing costs, people are not used to spending their scarce cash on a book — thus fulfilling the publisher's fear that printing local history books is not sustainable. Perhaps the place where one of these books got the most press was where it was featured in a music video "Historia" by the popular Tanzanian music star, Lady Jaydee.[7]

But what I most often hear from people in the Mara Region is that what they really want is access to my original interviews, to hear their own grandparents or respected elders who have now passed on tell the stories that are rarely heard anymore. There is a sense that these stories are being forgotten, and that even memories that I taped in 1995, twenty years ago, have not been passed on to the next generation. Youth who leave home early for school and work no longer sit with their elders, and have less connection with this material. Yet many are interested in learning what their elders valued in the past if they can access it through print or digital media. They don't have time or inclination to gather these materials themselves back home and there are few elders left to tell them. Even those who remain in the region seem keen to learn about the past, at least theoretically. The Tanzanian Department of Education's secondary school curriculum mandates teaching local histories. Yet there are few to no materials in the Mara Region available for this purpose, particularly because the ethnic configuration of the region is broken up into a diversity of small ethnic, linguistic and cultural groups. As one of the few scholars of this area, I want to make this material accessible back in the region in a useable, accessible and interactive form for future generations.

7 Lady Jaydee, "Historia", https://youtu.be/rt-TVyIx5R4

The Mara Cultural Heritage Digital Library (MCHDL)

With the increasing availability of new kinds of digital technologies it is now possible to imagine ways to return these collections of oral tradition to the communities or even families where they originated. My research in the Mara Region of Tanzania began with my 1995–1996 dissertation work, and continued through return trips in 2003, 2007, and 2010. At the center of my collection are recordings of more than five hundred hours of interviews, including hundreds of mini-audio-cassette tapes, photographs, videotapes, transcripts, field notes, genealogies, family histories, music, maps, manuscripts, dictionaries, and drawings, all in my possession. I have GPS points for historical sites overlaid on topographic maps, dictionaries put together by local intellectuals in the 1950s, and the transcripts and tapes of local historian Zedekia Oloo Siso's research, among other items. Few historical scholars have worked in this territory and so this is one of the few collections of material on the history of the region. In 2009 I conceived of the idea of constructing an online Mara Cultural Heritage Digital Library as a repository for these materials with the potential to add material from other scholars and local historians or students in the future. Since that time I have been slowly working through all of the obstacles involved in achieving that goal. The critical issues that I have faced in this project can be characterized as technological, economic, political and ethical; issues which can only be solved by building relationships with individuals, institutions and communities in a number of directions.

The nature of a digital project frequently dictates that the scholar who is most invested in the material does not possess the technological expertise or resources to execute the digital library alone. As someone trained in history I faced the fairly high bar of technical expertise, making it necessary to seek out, and even pay for, the advice and knowledge of others to even know how to start. I also teach at a small liberal arts college, Goshen College, that does not have a department set aside for this work, nor do they have much funding for a project of this scope. Scholars of "digital anthropology" have commented on the "new kinds of technological exclusivity" that is generated by digital media requiring continual updates, training, and new infrastructure (Geismar

2013: 255). Yet whatever issues I may have in putting together a digital library, doing this in Tanzania would not be possible, at least currently.

One of the first technical decisions was choosing the software platform from which to launch the project. Although a number of possibilities exist, we started with the Greenstone software which is a project out of New Zealand, supported by UNESCO, that seeks to create a free and robust system that can be run on older and slower computer systems with uneven internet connectivity such as might be found in rural Africa.[8] It is also a platform that can be modified and used by people with less specialized knowledge. There are also many other possibilities that have been innovated or used by indigenous communities, and more being developed each year.[9] So in the summer of 2011, with the support of Goshen College, I took the first concrete step forward in contracting a history student with technological skills to investigate and begin to construct the template for the Mara Cultural Heritage Digital Library based on his research on best practices in the field.[10]

I also had to work with students on digitizing and converting all of the research material into a digital format that could be used by the Greenstone system, including adding the metadata using a modified form of the standard Dublin Core protocol that makes it searchable and connects related files. With the help of small Goshen College grants, a number of people, including students, have worked on the tedious and time-consuming task of digitally recording all of the old mini-audio-cassettes and video (VCR) tapes that are experiencing rapidly deteriorating sound quality.[11] We have also had to work on converting an older database format that connects all of the pieces of the project together. A huge job for the future will be to insert tags into the oral material to be able to skip to those places based on keywords. Other students who know the local languages have been working on completing the transcripts. The collection is largely in local language

8 Greenstone Digital Library Software, http://www.greenstone.org

9 See for example Mukurtu, http://mukurtu.org

10 Thanks to Ted Maust, Kajungu Mturi and Oscar Kirwa who worked on this project over a number of summers, and Maple Scholars projects at Goshen College.

11 Thanks to Dean Anita Stalter and Goshen College's Maple Scholars program and Mininger Center grants for supporting this work over a number of years, and more recently to Mennonite.net.

mixed with Swahili and so would only be useful for people who know those languages. We have not done any translation except for making my interview notes available in English.

We still have a long way to go but now have a very limited sample collection up on the internet that can be viewed live, even though many of the audio features are not presently working. Currently, the site is located at maraculturalheritage.org.[12] The library is browsable by material type and a variety of metadata fields including name of person interviewed, people groups, place-names, topic, dates, or keywords. The user-interface is available in both Swahili and English and we are working to standardize personal and place names. Ultimately, the goal is to make the MCHDL accessible, maintainable, expandable and searchable. Although we are now using a standard Greenstone structure, in the future we will need a more user-friendly interface requiring extensive web design.

Even with this small sample set-up we still have a long way to go and a huge hurdle is economic constraints. Although Goshen College has been supporting this work with student assistance and the help of in-house technological expertise, the next step will take a much larger sum of money to have someone construct the final project as well as finish the digitizing and then load and tag all of the hundreds of files. I will need major grant money to make this possible. I tried to get grant funding from the American Council of Learned Societies and from the Africa-US Ambassadors Fund for Cultural Preservation at the US Embassy in Tanzania in 2011, neither of which came through. With cutbacks in funding for the humanities after the recession, one of the few sources of funding for this kind of project left is the National Endowment for the Humanities, which is highly competitive.

Another huge hurdle economically is to find a permanent server location for the material that can be routinely upgraded and serviced. Goshen College does not have this capacity and is only hosting on a temporary basis, at personal expense. Last summer I made contact with

12 http://maraculturalheritage.org. Thanks to Goshen College ITS and mennonite.net for hosting and working with the project until it can become self-supporting, and to Michael Sherer, Director of Technology at Goshen College for his support and willingness to travel with me to Michigan State University to think through the future of the project.

the African Online Digital Library and more specifically the MATRIX Center for Digital Humanities and Social Sciences at Michigan State University (MSU), which is hosting a variety of digital projects like the South African apartheid collection.[13] They were impressed by what I had already done on my own and encouraged me to find the funding to complete the project and then come to talk about migrating it to their system. However it would also mean moving from the Greenstone platform to the digital repository software that they developed called KORA. Putting this on a larger site is ultimately the only way that the project will be sustainable in the long run. MSU also noted that one of their projects in rural South Africa did not depend on internet access there, but on the distribution of CDs, which might be a more realistic possibility for the MCHDL in some locations.

Ethical and Political Dilemmas of Digital Return

But perhaps more troubling than overcoming the enormous technological and economic obstacles are the political or legal issues of "ownership" involved. The largest of these looming issues is that of permission or consent. Even if you have signed consent forms for an interview twenty years ago, no one at that time ever conceived of the possibility of the interview being made available on the internet to everyone. So does that mean one needs to go back and get new, signed consent from each informant, or their next of kin for the many that are deceased? What does that mean culturally when people are very suspicious of signing anything? Does it unintentionally signal that this is a highly profitable business? How do individual narrators give consent when the material is communal?[14] The government of Tanzania, through COSTECH, originally granted permission for my research and does not have guidelines to follow for consent. Therefore, in my 1995–1996 research, I followed a professional and personal set of ethical norms for working with my informants and their communities without signed forms — always being transparent about my research and giving back

13 Matrix MSU, Center for Digital Humanities and Social Sciences, http://www2.matrix.msu.edu. Thanks to Peter Limb and Catherine Foley for hosting us.

14 For similar reflections regarding a chance finding of a famous artist's song in a sound archive, see Camara *et al.* in this volume.

tapes and other written materials where possible. Oral history does not legally require a consent form even if it has become best practice. Yet the legal framework followed by most digital return projects hosted on the internet entails written consent or some kind of legal agreement.

Scholars and practitioners are beginning to discuss and find possible solutions to these pernicious questions around ownership and rights. Because of copyright law, when a scholar collects oral tradition that scholar essentially "owns" the materialscluding the recordings and transcriptions, and can choose to share them at will, whether or not any written or oral permission can be produced. When Aboriginal communities in Australia sought to gain some control over their heritage materials, they began to explore getting copyright and public domain rights to the material, as well as utilizing alternative "Creative Commons licenses", all within the framework of international intellectual property law. Because indigenous people were understood to be the "subject" of recordings rather than the "author" their legal rights to the material are precarious at best. Even if digital return allows those communities access, it does not give them legal ownership of the materials (Anderson and Christen 2013). In Australia, the Traditional Knowledge (TK) license and labels were used to address the problems of unequal power for indigenous communities in negotiating intellectual property rights.[15] Neither the interests of the scholar who wishes to make research material available, nor the communities that wish to protect it, are served by existing legal frameworks. Within the copyright law, all of these possible solutions depend on the identification of an individual author or an original work, whereas cultural heritage is by definition communal and not original to the one who tells it. There is an obvious need for reworking intellectual property rights law to accommodate and even facilitate digital return of cultural heritage (Anderson and Christen 2013: 107–108).

Jan Jansen, working on the countryside of Mali, suggests that we must move away from talking about permission, consent, and rights to find more culturally appropriate frameworks for working respectfully

15 Local Contexts (http://www.localcontexts.org) is the site for working out the TK arrangements. It is conceived under the World Intellectual Property Organization (WIPO) on Traditional Knowledge, Genetic Resources and Traditional Cultural Expressions (TKGRTCES).

with communities based on "permanent dialogue". Those involved in this work must recognize a "dynamic society context", that is constantly renegotiated, and will ultimately determine the nature and form of community control over cultural heritage. Perhaps instead of talking about "copyrights" we should be thinking in terms of "copy debts" — that is the debt that the scholar owes to the community for the work that has been cooperatively produced. Jansen (2012) suggests that making formal or legal agreements of ownership with the community will inevitably exclude some parts of the community and impose western definitions of ownership and individuality that are poorly suited to the context. Working through community relationships to facilitate this work may be more possible in Africa than in the US, Canada, and Australia where native groups have had to negotiate within the legal copyright framework. For example, the Intellectual Property Issues in Cultural Heritage (IPinCH) project from British Columbia is an international collaboration to "facilitate fair and equitable exchanges of knowledge relating to archaeology and cultural heritage", particularly through community-based participatory research for community-based initiatives.[16] Even with African projects, legal permissions may still be required, not by the partner community but by the national government or institutional projects onto which the digital library is migrated. In the short run I will work with communities in the Mara Region to develop some kind of a "fair-use" agreement that will give them rights over the digital library, along with the level of control they desire.[17]

Even given an agreement, a further question is whether the Digital Library should have Open Access on the internet or be closed with admittance by petition, and if so who would monitor the site. Some indigenous communities have solved this question by building in "cultural protocols" to define the level of access both within and outside the community. But if the material is on the internet it is difficult, if not impossible, to control how the information will be used. In some

16 IPinCh project description, http://www.sfu.ca/ipinch/about/project-description

17 Kim Christen, working in Australia, consented "to transfer my rights in the materials to the community, who is and really should be recognized as the legitimate authority". This is a release of copyright by the scholar to the community and signals "resistance to ongoing colonial privileges that the current copyright system perpetuates when it automatically vests ownership with me as the primary rights holder" (Anderson and Christen 2013: 120).

communities "Outreach Licenses" have been developed for use of material outside the community, which necessitated communication with the community and some expectation of reciprocity, even for educational use (Anderson and Christen 2013: 112, 115). These agreements depend on identifying and bringing together the various parties who have a stake in the heritage material for conversation. I hope to be able to return to the region and begin to work through some of these questions. I have already made contacts by email, both in the region and in Dar es Salaam through the University.

The fact that most of the material in the MCHDL is in local languages naturally limits who can use it, and makes it an important source of material for language preservation. This region is made up of many small ethnic groups speaking many different Bantu and Nilotic languages, meaning that few people outside the region could understand the audio files. As local languages quickly go out of daily use in preference for Swahili among the younger generation there is a higher danger of language extinction (Cha chom se nup [E. J. Smith] *et al.* 2013). The Summer Institute of Linguistics (SIL), working in the Mara Region to document and preserve indigenous languages, is interested in accessing audio recordings in the MCHDL as documentation of Mara's languages with original cultural material.[18] This will be an important partner for the MCHDL. British Columbia's First Peoples' Cultural Council established FirstVoices.com to record and digitize indigenous languages for their larger project of cultural revitalization (Cha chom se nup [E. J. Smith] *et al.* 2013: 195).[19]

In many digital return projects communities and scholars raise the issue of public access to culturally sensitive material. The oral traditions that I collected are considered communal property, but knowledge of those traditions is controlled by the male elders and given out to those who should know. The knowledge is not their individual property and yet they choose when and how to share or to keep the knowledge secret (Shetler 2002). I specifically avoided and did not solicit information that the elders considered secret and sensitive material. I often went with the elders to specific sites that are important in the origin or settlement traditions which provoked more historical memories. What I collected

18 Summer Institute of Linguistics, http://www.sil.org

19 See also First Peoples' Cultural Foundation, http://fpcf.ca and http://www.fpcc.ca

was the stories of origin, migration, nineteenth century conflict and famine, and their interactions with the colonial government and Serengeti National Park. This material, albeit public, is usually shared within groups of men who are responsible for passing the knowledge on, even as women are around to bring them food or beer. Some of my audio files include biographical material from the elders or information about their particular area of expertise, but again, as public information. Most of my interviews were conducted in a family homestead with neighbors, women, children and youth coming in and out as we talked. As far as I am aware none of this information would be harmful to anyone involved, although as an outsider I do not know that for sure. Whether the material should be all open for public access or some of it restricted will have to emerge in conversations with communities involved in the region (cf. Leopold 2013 for a sensitive case study).

And then there is the thorny question of who can speak for the community out of the many different parties involved, each with different interests in the digital library. Many of my original informants are now deceased, but even if they were alive the knowledge is not theirs individually. Their next of kin, clan or ethnic group could be identified, but who could speak for those groups and by what authority? This is a particularly tricky question in this heterarchical region without chiefs until the colonial period. The government as well as the university also has interest in preserving cultural heritage, particularly through the East Africana Library at the University of Dar es Salaam. One must acknowledge that there are a variety of voices and perspectives involved, even among people who live in the Mara Region that have some connection to the cultural material. Most digitization projects with material from indigenous people deal directly with "community gatekeepers", who make the decisions on behalf of others, without questioning the dynamics behind their authority. Because of easy access to digital collections, internal divisions and interests in the community must be engaged. Decisions on restricted or public access to cultural material has the potential to enhance the power of one group on the basis of gender, status or age, as well as lineage, over others. Of course issues of power and the potential for profit have always animated access to cultural heritage in museums, but now those dynamics have to be engaged more directly in conversation with the community on an ongoing basis, even after they gain access to the digital library (Leopold 2013: 88–89).

Even with permissions of some sort there is still the much larger epistemological question of how the translation and use of metadata in a digital library will affect the use and transmission of oral tradition (Geismar 2013: 258). Because digital information is so easily shared, copied and revised, the effects on traditional knowledge are potentially enormous, but at this point unknown. Many indigenous communities assume that access to digital collections will bring about the revitalization of cultural knowledge as well as encourage the on-going creation of new material, which they are taking deliberate steps to make happen (Bell *et al.* 2013: 7). But there is also the danger that oral tradition will become reified in one version rather than remaining a living dialogue of various perspectives and versions of the past. Recent scholarship in East Africa investigates the work of popular historians whose writing about "tradition" undergirds the exclusive claims of ethnic patriotism to land and the patriarchal authority of elders (Peterson and Macola 2009; Peterson 2012). My own research is now concerned with the very different kind of historical memory maintained by women in this region that does not follow ethnic lines (Shetler 2015). Thus, a digital library of cultural material may support a particular interpretation of the past and a particular claim to legitimacy. That is another reason why a broader range of community voices must be kept in dialogue.

The other political issue is that unless I have strong community partners who are willing to host the Digital Library and give locals access to it on their computers, the whole project will be untenable, as very few people have access to computers within their homes. With the contacts I already have in both the region and the nation, I have begun to write to people and institutions to ask if they are interested in hosting the Digital Library. These institutions include Secondary Schools up through a Theological College and a Teacher's Training College, Museums and Libraries, a Language School, Churches, NGOs, Community Resource Centers, the SIL, and the Government Cultural Office, as well as the University of Dar es Salaam East Africana Library collection. Most of these inquiries resulted in positive responses but perhaps without really knowing what it might entail. When I return to the region I want to explore with them what it would mean to have a set of CDs or internet access to the collection and whether they would have to charge a fee to be able to supervise its use.

In my most optimistic vision of how the library will be used I imagine local individuals, groups or students adding their own content to the site, commenting on what is already there, or doing more research, transcription or translation of the material. Scholars who publish from research in the region might also post links to their work. I hope that we can build some of this capacity into the library from the beginning. Many of the current projects with partner communities make use of the capacity for user-generated content and locally produced exhibits or other ways to share material (Bell *et al.* 2013: 6).[20] In this way the "digital return" becomes cyclical, rather than a one way process (Geismar 2013: 256).

Conclusion

Though huge hurdles remain in terms of funding, expertise and agreements, as well as my own stamina to continue this quest along with my teaching and research, I maintain that this is something that everyone who has collected oral tradition in Africa should consider. The questions about ultimate ownership of cultural heritage are the same whether we are talking about material artifacts or the spoken word. They are complex ethical questions that have no easy solutions and require a huge expenditure of resources and time without much return except the satisfaction of the community relationships. Sometimes the obstacles, both for the scholar and for the community, seem too high to make the endeavor worthwhile. Because of the expense involved in this kind of project it would be difficult for African nations to require this as part of permission to conduct research in oral tradition. And in the end it is quite possible that not many people would actually be interested in taking the time to search through and use the material. But in spite of that, it is something that should be there for the time, if and when, people become interested and begin to ask. Of course, ultimately it is up to the communities themselves to preserve their own heritage and that

20 For collaborative platforms see the Great Lakes Research Alliance for the Study of Aboriginal Arts and Culture, https://grasac.org/gks/gks_about.php or the Reciprocal Research Network, https://www.rrncommunity.org

does not depend on digital materials of any kind: "Collective memory belongs in people and place, not solely on electronic or digital tools" (Cha chom se nup [E. J. Smith] 2013: 192). It is my hope that the Mara Cultural Heritage Digital Library can serve as a tool to aid in passing on collective memory, but only as a small contribution in the larger scope of the process for Mara communities. Ethical and respectful sharing and exchange of knowledge through digital media is only possible by building relationships between scholars, community members and the digital material itself over the long term (Hennessey *et al.* 2013).

References

Anderson, J. and Christen, K. (2013) "'Chuck a Copyright on It': Dilemmas of Digital Return and the Possibilities for Traditional Knowledge Licenses and Labels", *Museum Anthropology Review* 7–1/2: 105–126.

Atalay, S. (2012) *Community-based Archaeology Research with, by, and for Indigenous and Local Communities* (Berkeley, University of California Press).

Bell, J. A., Christen, K. and Turin, M. (2013) "Introduction: After the Return (Digital Repatriation and the Circulation of Indigenous Knowledge)", *Museum Anthropology Review* 7–1/2: 1–21.

Brown, M. F. (2003) *Who Owns Native Culture?* (Cambridge, MA, Harvard University Press).

Cha chom se nup (Smith, E. J.), Heekkuus (Wells, V. C.) and Brand, P. (2013) "A Partnership between Ehattesaht Chinehkint, First Peoples' Culture Council, and First Peoples' Culture Council's Firstvoices Team to Build a Digital Bridge between the Past and the Future of the Ehattesaht Chinehkint Language and Culture", *Museum Anthropology Review* 7–1/2: 185–200.

Geismar, H. (2013) "Defining the Digital", *Museum Anthropology Review* 7–1/2: 254–263.

Hennessy, K., Lyons, N., Loring, S., Arnold, Ch., Joe, M., Elias, A., and Polk, J. (2013) "The Inuvialuit Living History Project: Digital Return as the Forging of Relationships between Institutions, People and Data", *Museum Anthropology Review* 7–1/2: 44–73.

Jansen, J. (2012) "'Copy Debts'? — Towards a Cultural Model for Researchers' Accountability in an Age of Web Democracy", *Oral Tradition* 27–2: 351–362.

Leopold, R. (2013) "Articulating Culturally Sensitive Knowledge Online: A Cherokee Case Study", *Museum Anthropology Review* 7–1/2: 85–104.

Lonetree, A. (2012) *Decolonizing Museums: Representing Native America in National and Tribal Museums* (Chapel Hill NC, University of North Carolina Press).

Mihesuah, D. A. (ed.) (2000) *Repatriation Reader: Who Owns American Indian Remains?* (Lincoln, University of Nebraska Press).

Peterson, D. R. (2012) *Ethnic Patriotism and the East African Revival* (Cambridge, Cambridge University Press).

Peterson, D. R. and Macola G. (eds.) (2009) *Recasting the Past: History Writing and Political Work in Modern Africa* (Athens, Ohio University Press).

Robertson, L. (2012) *Standing Up with Ga'axsta'las: Jane Cooke and the Politics of Memory, Church and Custom* (Vancouver, University of British Columbia Press).

Shetler, J. B. (2002) "The Politics of Publishing Oral Sources from the Mara Region, Tanzania", *History in Africa* 29: 413–426.

— (2003) *Telling Our Own Stories: Local Histories from South Mara, Tanzania* (Leiden, Brill) (republished in 2004 by Mkuki na Nyota Press, Dar es Salaam).

— (2007) *Imagining Serengeti: A History of Landscape Memory in Tanzania from Earliest Times to the Present* (Athens, Ohio University Press).

— (ed.) (2015) *Gendering Ethnicity in African Women's Lives* (Madison, University of Wisconsin Press).

Siso, Z(edekia) O. (2010) *Grasp the Shield Firmly, the Journey Is Hard: A History of Luo and Bantu Migrations to North, Mara (Tanzania) 1850–1950*, edited by Shetler, J. B. (Dar es Salaam, Mkuki na Nyota Press).

2. Technauriture as a Platform to Create an Inclusive Environment for the Sharing of Research

Russell H. Kaschula

Introduction — Objectives and Setting the Scene[1]

This chapter examines the importance of orality in rural communities using the paradigm of technauriture, which describes how technology, auriture[2] and literature intersect to transmit educational and other messages within communities. It uses oral literary research that has been conducted in the Eastern Cape region to show how technology can aid the data collection process, and how this technology can return such information to the communities from which it comes. This chapter also explores the process of orality fostered by community meetings, oral histories, oral poetry, beadwork, music and story-telling, and how this culture interacts with the recording process facilitated by modern technology. It will also consider the return of recorded oral material to educational and archival circles. These objectives are pursued using

1 The author acknowledges the contribution of Bongiwe Dlutu as well as the Rhodes team of Keiskammahoek researchers led by Lee Watkins. The financial assistance of the National Research Foundation (NRF) towards this research is hereby acknowledged. Opinions expressed and conclusions arrived at are those of the author and are not necessarily to be attributed to the NRF.

2 Auriture: a combination of aural (what we hear) and literature (from the written word), representing the relationship between orality and literacy.

 https://doi.org/10.11647/OBP.0111.02

empirical data collected at Tshani near Port St. Johns, an area falling within the Mankosi tribal authority in the Eastern Cape Province of South Africa. They are also considered in relation to the work of oral poet, Bongani Sitole who lived in Mqhekezweni village near Qunu and Mthatha, as well as against the backdrop of research conducted in Keiskammahoek, and at the Broster Beadwork Collection, now housed at Walter Sisulu University in Mthatha.

In recent years, oral history and literary research has been reintroduced to the Keiskammahoek community from an educational perspective. This includes research conducted into oral poetry (*izibongo*), especially the poetry produced by the late Bongani Sitole and the Broster Beadwork Collection, as well as oral literary research conducted within the communities living in specific areas of the Eastern Cape Province such as Keiskammahoek, Mqhekezweni, Mankosi, and the Port St. Johns area. Orality still proliferates in these areas and it is used for the documentation and dissemination of information in schools and archives, as I shall explore in this chapter. The Eastern Cape is largely inhabited by amaXhosa people and they live mainly in the previously "independent" homelands of Transkei and Ciskei respectively,[3] although many people migrated to the cities after the end of apartheid in 1994 (Kaschula 1997: 11). These former homelands are today regarded as disadvantaged; most people rely on government support grants and schools are often underresourced and the graduation rates are very low. The primary technological devices used by people in the villages and rural areas are the radio, the mobile phone and, to some extent, the television. The isiXhosa radio station *Umhlobo Wenene* (*True Friend*), for example, has 4.6 million listeners; it is the second largest radio station in South Africa and it covers eight out of nine provinces.[4] This chapter seeks to understand how mobile phones and the radio can contribute to support learning in an educational context in which even television sets are relatively uncommon.

Mankosi's twelve villages are inhabited by amaXhosa people and are situated in the Ngqeleni district in the former Transkei region.

3 These were separate and so-called independent areas of South Africa that were inhabited by black people under apartheid. It was part of the divide-and-rule policy of the apartheid regime at that time.

4 http://www.umhlobowenenefm.co.za

Mqhekezweni is situated next to Qunu which is about forty kilometres from Mthatha, while Keiskammahoek is near East London in the old Ciskei homeland. Even though these areas have many problems, their remoteness encourages people to hold on to their cultural values. Elders in the villages are often not well educated in the Western sense (for instance, most cannot read and write, and many do not speak English). They use traditional knowledge to guide their children and families, and are still able to narrate folktales, tell stories of their own experiences during the apartheid era, and describe how they live in the present time. Theirs is largely an oral culture underpinned by the isiXhosa language.

The danger of orality is that the narrated story may change over time and no longer accurately reflect what was initially said. Issues around the notion of "accuracy" are further explored by Bidwell and Siya (2013). The context in which stories and poetry are narrated has altered due to changes in lifestyle. This means that the interpretation of the telling of, and listening to, old stories has also changed, and it is much less likely to communicate the meanings that were originally intended. The use of technology and technauriture can assist in more accurately recording such events for posterity and returning them to the community. According to Starr, "The oral history movement may be perceived as a conscious effort to utilize technology — not only the tape recorder, but [...] microforms, the computer and other tools of the age" (1984: 5). Arguably, today these new tools would include mobile phones, tablets, video recorders, computers and the internet.[5]

Orality and technology are now integrally intertwined. It remains to be seen just how this link will ultimately influence the performance and the reception, dissemination and archiving of oral forms.

---

5 Such an approach has been validated by the technologized work of the *Verba Africana* Series, for example. In 2012, I noted that: "Further examples of ground-breaking work in terms of technauriture would be the *Verba Africana* series which has been developed at the University of Leiden (Netherlands) as part of the project *Verba Africana; E-learning of African languages and Oral Literatures: DVDs and Internet Materials.* The aim of this project is to document African oral genres (poems, narratives, songs and so on) for both teaching and research purposes [...]. There is also the project Encyclopaedia of Literatures and Languages of Africa (ELLAF) supported by various organisations and coordinated by French scholars. This project provides an online encyclopaedia devoted to the dissemination, archiving and study of African oral literature (http://ellaf.huma-num.fr)" (Kaschula 2012a: 236).

The Importance of Orality

Many forms of orality persist in rural and urban areas, from listening to the radio as an aural experience to performances by oral poets (*iimbongi*). With regard to the latter, it is especially within the context of contemporary amaXhosa life that the *imbongi* operates. Traditionally, the most recognized *imbongi* were those who were attached to the chiefs and who produced oral poetry in their honor, normally located within rural areas. But today the tradition has also moved into the contemporary political arena, where important figures are praised in the same way that traditional chiefs are praised (Kaschula 2002). For example, Bongani Sitole from Mqhekezweni was the first poet to perform for Nelson Mandela after his release from prison in 1991. Indeed, oral poetry played a vital role in the struggle for independence prior to 1994, thereby contributing to the continued importance of orality in South African society (Gunner 1999: 50). In a similar way, the folktale and other forms of orality have adapted to contemporary village life. Arguably the oral word lives alongside the technologized word: orally performed folktales and television and radio programs espouse a similar tradition. The work of performer Gcina Mhlophe[6] is particularly well-known in this technologized arena as she previously presented story-telling programs on the South African Broadcasting Corporation (SABC) television channels. One can also consider the oral poet, Zolani Mkiva, who has won numerous international awards for his performances and who became known as "The President's Poet" or *imbongi yesizwe* ("The Poet of the Nation"). His website (http://poetofafrica.com) is a good example of technauriture and the importance of orality in contemporary South Africa.

Technauriture and the Orality/Literacy Debate

There is vibrant debate around orality and oral literature in South Africa and throughout the world. "If one portrays orality and literacy as incompatible and different, rather than forming part of the same continuum, then one is left with images of literacy versus illiteracy,

6 http://www.gcinamhlophe.co.za

civilization versus non-civilization, structure versus non-structure and so on" (Kaschula 2002: 66). This debate is exemplified by the conflicting views of Finnegan (1988) and Ong (1982), where Finnegan suggests the two forms interact, while Ong sees them as totally separate, with literacy replacing orality. The new political order in South Africa has introduced a renewed pride in what it is to be African, hence there has been a revival in the status and role of oral literature. This form of literature is fast taking its rightful place alongside written literature and is now studied in schools and universities. Furthermore, it is used in an innovative way to teach people about HIV and AIDS, agriculture, family planning and so on (see Dauphin-Tinturier in Kaschula 2001: 54). The didactic or educational nature of this literature means that it can be studied for its own sake and it can be used elsewhere in South Africa in more practical contexts, for example the use of folktales to impart knowledge to young pregnant teenage mothers by the Eastern Cape Health Department (Zakaza 2014). But if orality is to serve any long-term purpose, it must be taught and recognized as a dynamic, living tradition which has much to offer.

Oral literature in South Africa finds itself at the centre of the debate about what literature is, and how it is to be taught. The relevance of the oral word alongside the written word is the focus of discussion worldwide. Coplan talks of extending terms such as orature and oral literature to "auriture" which, according to him, encapsulates not only the oral and the written, but the aural as well (1994: 8). In a similar way, Gunner discusses the mixing of genres, the orality-literacy debate, and so on (1989: 49). In an extensive article in which she reviews the state of oral literature in Africa since the publication of her famous book *on the subject* (*Oral Literature in Africa*, 1970; 2012[7]), Finnegan states the following in regard to the term "oral literature":

> My own inclination would definitely be to keep it. [...] To me the advantages mostly outweigh the costs [...]. It highlights the creative, aesthetic qualities and the significance of heightened and formalised linguistic activities in a cultural [sic] recognised setting [...] the term

7 The revised and expanded 2012 edition of *Oral Litarature in Africa*, published by Open Book Publishers, is Open Access and freely available to read and download at http://dx.doi.org/10.11647/OBP.0025. To date the book in its free editions has been accessed more in Africa than in any other continent. See also Turin: 147 in this volume.

> also draws the study of Africa into the terminology and scholarship of international comparatives study [...] (1992: 42).

In terms of contemporary oral forms, it would seem that there are three areas of prominence in South Africa. These are: contemporary stories (including media such as the internet, radio and television); entrepreneurial oral art which is sold for capital gain; and oral poetry. The three are linked by commercial value. Forms such as riddles, idioms and proverbs play a less prominent role and are often incorporated into other genres, for example, stories.

Finnegan (1977 and 2012) and Ong (1982) have long debated the nature of orality and its relationship with technologies such as writing systems. To a degree they represent two sides of the same coin. Both accept the innate value of oral cultures and oral tradition. Ong (1982: 9) states that "human beings in primary oral cultures, those untouched by writing in any form, learn a great deal and possess and practice great wisdom, but they do not 'study'". Finnegan however is emphatic in her recognition of the role of oral poetry, and by extension orality, and its innate value to human society: "it is difficult to argue that they [oral poets] should be ignored as aberrant or unusual in human society, or in principle outside the normal field of established scholarly research. In practice there is everything to be gained by bringing the study of oral poetry into the mainstream of work on literature and sociology" (Finnegan 1977: 2). Perhaps Finnegan's statement could now be adapted to include not only work on literature and sociology, but also to modern-day technologies.

It is against this backdrop of the interplay of orality and the influence of technology that the term technauriture has been coined (Kaschula 2004a; Kaschula and Mostert 2011). In terms of the etymological roots, the "techn" represents technology, the "auri" is derived from the word auriture, whilst the "ture" represents literature in the more conventional sense. Auriture, used by Coplan, implies the use of a range of senses in one's appreciation of the oral word: hearing, speaking and the more abstract aesthetic analysis of the word (1994: 9). Auriture has been suggested in place of orature, orality or oraural, the latter a term used by Kishani (2001: 27).

Technauriture attempts to embrace the implicit dichotomies that Ong and Finnegan acknowledge, and to place the debate regarding orality firmly in a twenty-first century discourse; one that will offer a coherent nomenclature that can seamlessly traverse various disciplines to locate orality in an interdisciplinary paradigm that promotes the capture, nurture and harnessing of orality, oral histories and oral traditions. The term encompasses orality and extends beyond it, which allows other disciplines to address issues of orality and oral tradition without being constrained by the nature, definition and applicability of orally based knowledge and knowledge systems in relation to their particular academic discourse.

Kaschula (2004a, 2004b, 2009, 2012c) and Kaschula and Mostert (2011) define technauriture as an attempt to capture the modalities associated with the three-way dialectic between primary orality, literacy and technology, thus moving the debate into a more sophisticated realm that expands what has essentially been a tension between orality, writing and the use of technology in re-inventing the oral word. This discussion now includes the implications of technology as a general and alternative category. The term includes all technologies that can be brought to bear on the issues of orality, oral history, community meetings with headmen and oral traditions more generally. It also encompasses the implications of the application of technology to contexts that should be characterized by a sympathetic perspective towards orally based cultures. This is an attempt to recognize that human culture has evolved to be more aware of the implications of technological advances.

Case Studies in Orality

What follows are case studies of recorded orality in villages in Mankosi and surrounding areas. Arguably, the mere recording of this material transports it into the realm of technauriture. All case studies were part of a technology design project instigated by researchers who are not isiXhosa, some of whom have spent very little time in Mankosi and who sought to design and deploy prototype technologies to support local communication (Bidwell *et al.* 2013).

The first two cases occurred very early in the process of generating data to inform the design of technologies. Local researchers, aged fourteen to eighty years old, recorded over fifty items in total, which featured some sixty people in interviews, conversations, storytelling, and presentations. The external researchers were not provided with written translations at the time, rather they were provided with two video recordings. This included the original video recording (O) and a video recording (T) of one of the local researchers, who had recorded O, watching and listening to O and orally translating the spoken words into English. Local researchers prepared the translation, T, within three days of making the original recording, O.

The first study involved a story told by a village elder, an old and respected woman filmed seated on a grass mat inside her rondaval (the mud-brick traditional dwellings that comprise most homesteads). Two local researchers were involved in the recording. This is in line with the commonly held definition of orality as a communicative event which is handed down from generation to generation by respected orators who are drawn from the older generation.

Recorded Folk Tale: Capture and Dissemination

Once upon a time!

There was a woman who had only two daughters, the first one was Dengekazi and the second was Qhaqha. One day the woman sent her daughters to fetch *inkciyo* (a garment worn by virgin girls as underwear which has a beaded front) from her brother's wife in a village far from theirs. She gave her children food to eat on the way and instructed, "You will walk a very long distance my children and when you are about to reach the village you will see a junction; one will be a road to the left and on the right you will see a walkway. Please do not use the walkway; take the big road then you will get to your uncle's place, do you get me beautiful daughters?"

The daughters nodded their heads, as a sign that they had understood their mother. They left their home; it became dark while they were still walking, and suddenly they approached the two-way junction, a road on the left and walkway on the right. They stood and argued as to which way to go.

Dengekazi: "We must take the walkway."

Qhaqha: "But mother said we must use the road to the left and that will take us straight to uncle's place."

Dengekazi: "Mother said we must turn to the right and I won't argue with you as you are young."

Dengekazi took the walkway while Qhaqha was standing, left puzzled by her sister's decision. She then decided to follow her older sister because she was scared to walk alone in the dark, *"Khawume khe ndilandele isidenge sikaMama"* ("Wait then, let me follow my Mother's fool"). They walked until midnight and then they saw a light in a one-hut homestead. They decided to stay there and get a place to sleep. They went inside and found a woman called Nomlenzana; she had one arm, one leg, and one eye. Nomlenzana asked the children, "Why are you here, little girls?" Qhaqha answered, "We want a place to sleep; we are from a village far away; mother sent us to uncle's place but we lost our way."

Nomlenzana replied, "Little girls, this is a dangerous place; a woman who owns this hut is Nomahamle, a cannibal; she hunts and eats people. She has eaten my other parts but could not finish because I am fat and she always comes home late with her stomach full. You can sleep in the big bucket over there, but be cautious; when she asks who you are, you tell her you are her brother's daughters; when she is sleeping you will hear a very big noise of a man who sings inside her stomach; at that time you must try to escape. When she comes home you will hear a big wind and noise."

Dengekazi and Qhaqha went inside the big bucket and they closed it. In a minute they heard a big wind blowing, Nomahamle entered the hut. She was very tired and drowsy, but she sensed that there are people inside the hut except Nomlenzana, and she asked, "Who are you, you must be fat?"

Qhaqha answered, "We are your brother's daughters."

The cannibal continued, "But my brother's daughters cannot sleep in the bucket, why are you hiding from me? Anyway sleep, I will see you in the morning."

Qhaqha could not sleep; she heard loud music and knew Nomahamle was sleeping. She then woke Dengekazi, so that they can escape. Qhaqha opened the bucket quietly. They ran as fast as they could. They ran in the desert, they could not hide. When they were far they wanted to slow down but they saw smoke behind them, it was Nomahamle with a shining axe. They ran, and saw a big tall tree. They climbed; Nomahamle tried to climb, but she fell. Nomahamle then tried to cut the tree down so that the girls can fall. She chopped and chopped... When the tree was about to fall a voice of the Drongo bee-catcher bird called and sang:

Ntengu, ntengu macetyana, hazuba. ("The drongo (bee-catcher) bird has a plan.") *Abantwana babantu benze ntoni na?* ("What have the people's children done?")

Yima mth'omkhulu uthi gomololo. ("Stand up straight big tree.")

The tree stood again, and every time the tree started to fall the bird sang. Nomahamle looked up and saw it and she swallowed it. When she was about to chop the tree again, men who were hunting animals with dogs came along. The dogs ate Nomahamle and the men took the girls. Among the men there was Qhaqha's uncle. He took them to his home, gave them food, and they slept. The following day, their uncle's wife gave them *inkciyo* to give to their mother. She gave them directions and told Dengekazi to listen to Qhaqha this time and to obey her. They left the village and arrived safely at their home. The end!

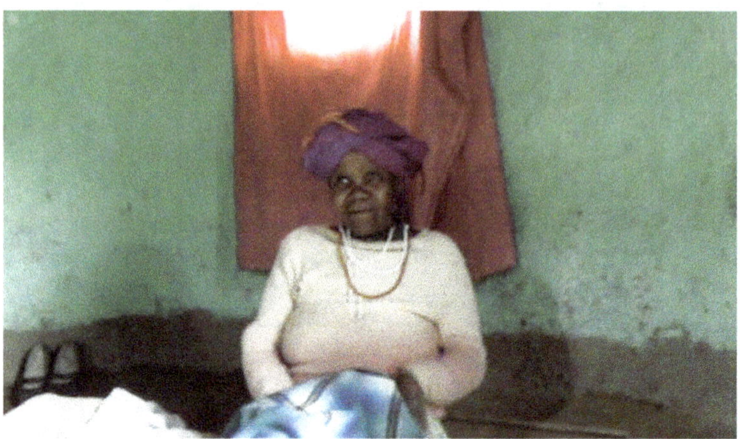

Fig. 2.1 Mama Mdzolo — a storyteller who narrated the above folktale. Photograph by Bongiwe Dlutu.

Arguably, recording and translation allows the transportation of this folktale to a wider audience as a result of making use of modern recording technologies. For someone who is not from Mankosi the material offers insight into local history, myths, and values. The linguistic translation depicts stylistic aspects of communication while the video, O, illustrates qualities of speaking, listening, and recording. It also reflects the relationships between speaker, listener and camera person. The video-recorded translation, T, illustrates qualities of speaking and listening, and their relationship to media or technauriture. For instance, the video, O, focuses entirely on the elder woman speaking and the only other visual content is the mat on which she sits, her blanket which she sometimes picks up and handles to illustrate a feature of her stories, and a pair of shoes neatly propped up against the wall of the rondaval behind her (Figure 2.1). A simple written translation of the story would not have communicated all that the video, photographic and vocal translation did, and the recording medium offers the opportunity to disseminate the story widely. The extralinguistic features such as gestures are therefore captured for posterity by the camera. The picture of the storyteller can also live on through a technologized archive which can be accessed by future generations.

Recorded Oral History as Social Commentary

The second study is a directly translated interview with a Mankosi male elder. This was captured on video prior to transcription and translation. Again, the use of technology allows societal insights to be captured. Such insights may also be important in creating an understanding of society at a particular time in history. It creates a visual experience which again can be archived using modern technologies.

> In our times, long before you were born, boys were wearing *izitshuba*. They were not allowed to walk with circumcised men because they would not be allowed to talk about similar topics. Boys like chatting about girlfriends and unimportant things, like stealing and killing pigs for fun. Even girls were not allowed to walk with married women. Gender roles were very important in teaching what to do and what you are not supposed to do.
>
> Women were not allowed to reveal what is happening in the *Intonjane* (entering womanhood) ritual in the same way as circumcised men were not allowed to talk about initiation to those who had not yet been circumcised.
>
> Long ago a man would go to *eGoli* (Gauteng) to seek work on the mines and when he came back the first time he would get circumcised and his father would secure him a wife. The working man was not allowed to take any money from his wages or salary except transport fare from Gauteng to Transkei. We used to keep the money in our underwear when we were on the train home, so that thieves didn't find it as crime was very high on the train. Even if you had a wife, you had to give money to your father. The wife was not allowed to see how much her husband gets as a salary. After giving the money to your father, he would ask you to count the money with him and his wife (your mother) standing next to him. He would sort the money and take out money for food, for buying cattle and then give you a small amount to buy yourself tobacco or traditional beer. When it was time to go back to Gauteng then your father would provide you with your train fare.
>
> I remember in other years there was a disease called *Ingqakaqa*. It left people's faces with holes. Only doctors knew the cause of this disease and there was no cure for it. In other years it was very difficult for us to grow crops because of the locusts that were everywhere. I don't know which year it was because I am uneducated; we name things including babies according to events that happened. That's how educated people trace an event. A baby who was born in the year of locust was called Nonkumbi. A locust in Xhosa is called *Inkumbi*.

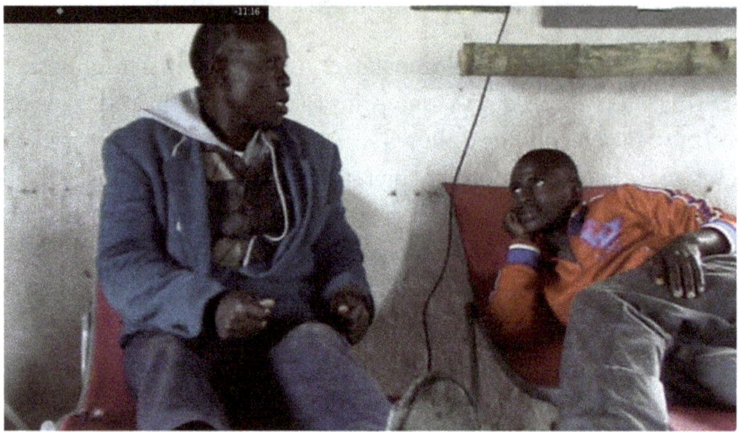

Fig. 2.2 Narrator (known affectionately as Tata Sparks) telling the story of his life in Johannesburg, as documented and transcribed above. Photograph by Bongiwe Dlutu.

This video as well as the photographs can be archived for years to come: it captures an oral history which can then be returned to the community and which can be used for further research. Such narratives illuminate particular historical periods. In this case, one gains insight into the migrant labour system which was used under the apartheid regime, in which men were sent away from their families to work primarily on the gold mines in the present-day Gauteng Province. This sort of data collection therefore enables the opportunity for such oral histories to be preserved and disseminated among future generations using contemporary technology.

Recorded Orally-Based Court Case

The diagram below depicts participants in a traditional court case. These cases are heard orally and decided orally, but decisions are recorded in written form by the Chief's Secretary.[8] Examples of court cases involve pregnancy damages, the misuse of natural community resources such

8 Rural communities are run by Chiefs, someone (normally the eldest son) who inherits this position from his forefathers. In certain instances a Headman is appointed and this is not an inherited position, i.e. where the Chieftancy is not already in place.

as building sand, fishing without appropriate licenses, or unsustainably and illegally harvesting sea mussels. Court cases can also involve the misuse of community trust funds and other infringements.

Traditional court case participants	Traditional court case participants
Ward councillor (part of the jury)	Headman/Chief (officiates at court cases) Offender and victim (seated in front, normally on the ground)
Ward committee members (part of the jury)	Sub-headmen (part of a jury)
Church leaders (part of the jury)	Headman/Chief
Headman's secretary (recording officer; takes the minutes and records the decision)	Sub-headmen and witnesses
Community members (who came to listen)	Community members (who came to listen)

Recordings made by participants of court cases, using the Audio Repository, is a good example of an ethnographic study where participants form part of what Hymes refers to as an ethnographic framework in order to analyze a communicative event (Hymes 1962: 101). Saville-Troike supports this approach by stating that the ethnography of speaking posits language as a socially situated cultural form (Saville-Troike 1982: 2–3).

The above diagram shows that court cases are held as communicative events, and are inclusive of all members of the community who are called on to voice their opinions in an inclusive way prior to a verdict being reached. This allows for any verdict to have the approval of the community. These court cases are examples of powerful orality, in which decisions are made about individuals. Such decisions are then set down in writing or, in the case of the Audio Repository, audio recordings, through technology such as electronic tablets, thereby facilitating a move towards technauriture by capturing and disseminating of orally based material.

The Broster Beadwork Collection

A further contemporary example of the digitization, archiving and dissemination of oral art is the Broster Beadwork Collection of the Eastern Cape Province. Beadwork is indeed a form of oral literature as it is a skill which is handed down from one generation to another by word of mouth in the same way that other oral literary forms are handed down orally. Contemporary bead makers have also created a niche for themselves as entrepreneurial art makers, selling their beadwork to the general public. The Broster Collection could have marked the beginnings of this process, though it is noted by Broster that it was sometimes difficult to acquire these items as the local community was often not keen to sell them to her (interview with the author, December 1992). This magnificent, authentic and original collection was acquired by Joan Broster in the mid-1900s. The beadwork dates back to 1875. It is carefully catalogued and was purchased in 1992 by the former University of Transkei, now Walter Sisulu University, to be housed in the Bureau for African Research and Documentation. For many years thereafter this beadwork lay in storage.

The collection began when Joan Broster's grandfather pioneered a trading business in the Engcobo district of the Transkei region in 1875. Four Clarke generations lived among the Thembu before Broster, as a young bride, moved to the village of Qebe in 1952 to run a family trading store. There she studied abaThembu traditions and developed a passion for their beadwork. Broster accumulated and documented her extensive collection, particularly the local costumes and beadwork of abaThembu, which demonstrated how beadwork mapped social identity within this isiXhosa-speaking community (Lusu 2015). She also used her contacts with the network of traders in the region to collect beadwork from other Xhosa-speaking groups, such as amaMpondo, amaMpondomise, amaBomvana, amaGcaleka, and a refugee amaXesibe group that had settled among the abaThembu in the early 1800s and adopted their customs, dress code and way of life.

With the advent of technauriture, this beadwork collection is again in the process of "coming alive" as part of the "Specifically Declared Broster Beadwork Collection". This is a collaboration between the National Department of Arts and Culture as well as the Walter Sisulu University. A climate-controlled building has been built in order to house the collection, which can now be returned to the community via technauriture and contemporary archival systems. Interviews that I conducted with the late Joan Broster can now be digitized and used to support the archive via screenings through television monitors. Newspaper interviews and books published by Broster can be used to augment the archive and add to the value of the project once digitized.

Extract from the 1992 interview with Joan Broster. Duration: 7.40 minutes.[9]

The Broster Collection has resulted in necessary engagement between the university and rural communities of the Eastern Cape, and will undoubtedly facilitate research in indigenous knowledge systems that will benefit both the scientific agenda and the communities from which this knowledge was derived. It is also envisaged that postgraduate research in the form of M.A. and Ph.D. research (based on the collection) would serve to develop the academic potential of the project and to create awareness around the importance of preserving our heritage through technology. This is an ongoing initiative. The digitization and cataloguing of this archive, the creation of a building to house the collection, and the easy access afforded to the public follows cutting-edge archival procedure, creating educational links between collector, academic and community.

9 This embedded video is also available at http://www.openbookpublishers.com/product/590#resources

Digitization and Dissemination: Further Comment

It is especially within the context of contemporary amaXhosa life that the *imbongi* or oral poet operates. For example, as indicated earlier, Bongani Sitole from Mqhekezweni was the first poet to perform for Nelson Mandela after his release from prison in 1991. In a similar way, the folk tale and other forms of orality have also adapted to contemporary village life, including in Keiskammahoek, Mankosi and other research sites. Technology such as the printed word, television, mobile phones and the internet allow this material to be re-accessed by the community from an educational and entertainment point of view.

In this chapter I have outlined and defined the notion of technauriture and how it can apply to a rural community. Analysis of communicative events such as a folk tale, social commentary, oral poetry, and beadwork, as well as traditional court cases, have been used to depict the emerging relationship between orality, literacy and technology. The analysis suggests that involving locally-based researchers from the community in communicative events, by translating and interpreting them, and in research design decisions, can lead to technologies that return the oral word to rural communities, but might also enrich the potential for technauriture. In Keiskammahoek this involves using community members as research assistants and interpreters to assist students and academics when collecting research data, thereby creating employment. These communicative events in Keiskammahoek include the following: oral poetry performances, story-telling or folk tale performances, dances and songs sung by diviners, games played by children, women singing traditional songs, village choirs performing, traditional instruments being played such as the harp or *uhadi* and the playing of traditional home-made guitars as well as mouth organs, and the singing of initiation songs by young boys. All of these performances, once recorded, are digitized for safe-keeping and dissemination within the community by the International Library for African Music (ILAM) where such digitization facilities exist. Likewise, the Broster Beadwork Collection will attract postgraduate students to further document the beadwork, the role of beadwork in society and the societal value of the specific beads at hand.

In summary, returning the oral word to communities, or else the artifact produced via oral messages handed down over generations, has been done in a number of ways. Firstly, there is the publication of books which are used in the education system. Bongani Sitole's transcribed and translated oral poems were published in the book *Qhiwu-u-u-la! Return to the Fold* which was reprinted in 2006[10] and made freely available to schools in the community. Furthermore, there is the use of websites (which can be accessed via mobile phones) to record and disseminate this material, as well as the digitization of recordings which are then uploaded onto television sets, for example at Cata village in Keiskammahoek. This is done in the community centre where members of the community can see themselves in action and where the material can be used for educational purposes.

Conclusion

> The need to develop and harness indigenous knowledge systems across the developing world is a central aspect of the maintenance of cultural identity, while widening the exposure to the traditions and customs of indigenous societies through technauriture will ensure that the momentum of globalization is of benefit to all the world's communities (Kaschula 2012b: 36).

The analysis in this chapter suggests that the researcher, the material, the subject, the community and various technologies are now becoming intertwined. This allows for innovative technological links between the researchers and the material, and it furthermore presents ways of disseminating research data back to relevant communities.

10 By Via Afrika Publishers with funding from the Foundation of Human Rights sponsored by the European Union.

References

Bidwell, N. J. and Siya, M. J. (2013) *"Situating Asynchronous Audio" Proceedings of INTERACT'13, Lecture Notes in Computer Science* (Berlin, Springer Verlag), https://doi.org/10.1007/978-3-642-40477-1_3

Coplan, D. (1994) *In the Time of Cannibals: The Word Music of South Africa's Basotho Migrants* (Johannesburg, Witwatersrand University).

Dauphin-Tinturier, A. (2001) "AIDS and Girls' Initiation in Northern Zambia", in: Kaschula R. H. (ed.) *African Oral Literature. Functions in Contemporary Contexts* (Cape Town, New Africa Books): 54–71.

Dunaway, D. K. and Baum W. K. (eds.) (1984) *Oral History. An Interdisciplinary Anthology* (Nashville, The American Association for State and Local History in Cooperation with the Oral History Association).

Finnegan, R. (1970) *Oral Literature in Africa* (Oxford, Clarendon Press). Revised and expanded edition (Cambridge, Open Book Publishers, 2012), http://dx.doi.org/10.11647/OBP.0025

— (1977) *Oral Poetry: Its Nature, Significance and Social Context* (Cambridge, Cambridge University Press).

— (1988) *Orality and Literacy* (Oxford, Basil Blackwell).

Gunner, L. (1999) "Remaking the Warrior? The Role of Orality in the Liberation Struggle and in Post-Apartheid South Africa", in: Brown, D. (ed.) *Oral Literature and Performance in Southern Africa* (Oxford/Cape Town/Athens OH, James Currey/David Philip/Ohio University Press): 50–60, https://doi.org/10.1080/1013929x.1995.9677957

Hymes, D. H. (1962) "The Ethnography of Speaking", in: Gladwin T. and Sturtevant, W. C. (eds.) *Anthropology and Human Behavior* (Washington DC, Anthropological Society of Washington).

Kaschula, R. H. (1997) *Xhosa* (The Heritage Library of African Peoples) (New York, The Rosen Publishing Group Inc.).

— (2002) *The Bones of the Ancestors are Shaking: Xhosa Oral Poetry in Context* (Cape Town, Juta Press).

— (2004) "Imbongi to Slam: The Emergence of a Technologised Auriture", *Southern African Journal of Folklore Studies* 14–2: 45–58.

— (2012a) "Teaching Oral Literature in the 21st Century", in: Gohrisch J. and Grunkemeier, E. (eds.) *Listening to Africa. Anglophone African Literatures and Cultures* (Heidelberg, Universitätsverlag Winter GmbH): 213–334.

— (2012b) "Technauriture: Southern African Poetry in the Digital Age", in: Gehrmann, S. and Veit-Wild, F. (eds.) *Conventions and Conversions. Generic Innovations in African Literatures* (Trier, WVT Wissenschaftlicher Verlag): 25–36.

Kaschula, R. H., Matyumza, M. and Sitole, B. (1995/2006) *Qhiwu-u-u-la!! Return to the Fold!! A Collection of Bongani Sitole's isiXhosa Oral Poetry* (Cape Town, Via Afrika).

Kaschula, R. H. and Mostert, A. (2009) "Analyzing, Digitizing and Technologizing the Oral Word: The Case of Bongani Sitole", *Journal of African Cultural Studies* 21–2: 159–176, https://doi.org/10.1080/13696810903259384

— (2011) "From Oral Literature to Technauriture. What's in a Name?" Occasional paper, World Oral Literature Project (University of Cambridge, UK).

Kishani, B. T. (2001) "On the Interface of Philosophy and Language in Africa: Some Practical and Theoretical Considerations", *African Studies Review* 44–3: 27–45, https://doi.org/10.2307/525592

Lusu, V. (2015) *The Specifically Declared Broster Beadwork Collection* (Mthatha, Walter Sisulu University).

Ong, W. J. (1982) *Orality and Literacy: The Technologizing of the Word* (London, Routledge).

Saville-Troike, M. (1982) *The Ethnography of Communication. An Introduction* (Oxford, Basil Blackwell Ltd.), https://doi.org/10.1002/9780470758373

Starr, L. (1984) "Oral History", in: Dunaway, D. K. and Baum, W. K. (eds.) *Oral History. An Interdisciplinary Anthology* (Nashville TN, American Association for State and Local History in Cooperation with the Oral History Association): 3–26, https://doi.org/10.1093/ohr/12.1.172

Zakaza, N. (2014) "IsiXhosa Storytelling (iintsomi) as an Alternative Medium for Maternal Health Education in Primary Healthcare in the Eastern Cape", M.A. thesis, Rhodes University (Grahamstown).

3. From Restitution to Redistribution of Ewe Heritage: Challenges and Prospects

Kofi Dorvlo

Introduction[1]

This chapter presents the rituals of Hogbetsotso, a migration festival of the Anlo-Ewe people, which is celebrated every year as the re-enactment of the migration of Ewe ancestors from present-day Togo to Ghana. Ewe believe that the rituals wash away the ill-feeling and negative thoughts capable of destroying the harmony of the state. The rituals include Dɔɖeɖe, or the physical removal of dirt in the community; Aƒekpɔkplɔ, mental cleansing to facilitate the unity of the state; Nugbidodo, an act of purification to reconcile the people; Tsiƒoƒoɖi, a libation prayer; and Abaɖoɖo, a ritual to remember the departed souls of the community by reciting their names and their deeds, asking them to intercede between the dead and the living. In these rituals, gods and ancestors are invoked to protect and reconcile the people. The ancestors are also expected to give guidance and support for the years ahead.

This chapter explores the documentation and sharing of heritage materials as a response to those Ewes who feel that the knowledge of the Hogbetsotso is disintegrating. An increasing number of people video-record the festival as cultural heritage to be kept for the future, often selling the recordings as documentary material. This chapter also calls for the creation of a "Heritage week" for both locals and tourists, and

1 I am most grateful to the reviewers for their comments and suggestions.

 https://doi.org/10.11647/OBP.0111.03

suggests that video materials be archived in local museums. The central issue is how are these rituals associated with the Hogbetsotso festival, and how they can be preserved and shared to make them relevant and beneficial to the Anlo State, and to the Ewe people, in a globalized world with competing cultural contacts and influences.

The Anlo are one of the Ewe groups who, in the early seventeenth century, migrated from the walled city of Notsie (in the present-day Republic of Togo) and settled in the territory of what is now the present-day Republic of Ghana. The Anlo-Ewe now mainly occupy the South Eastern sector of the Volta Region of Ghana, as well as other parts of the country. According to Gayibor and Aguigah (2005), Agokoli succeeded his father Ago as the King of Notsie and his reign was marked by singular violence and tyranny, which were the primary cause of Ewe migrations. Amenumey (1997) supports the migration narrative with archeological findings which point to the fact that Ewe migrations began in present-day Benin in the eleventh century, settling in Ghana in the seventeenth century. On arriving at their present location, the Anlo-Ewe instituted many rituals to preserve the integrity of their state. These rituals have become a part of the Hogbetsotso festival, with the objective of purging the state of all possible forms of evil.

The Ewe people believe that God is the Supreme Being and the creator of the world, including all of the people and things that dwell in it.[2] They therefore hold the firm view that His powers transcend theirs and that He has the unique attribute of omnipresence. They feel that God is distant from them, but that He is the one who gives the spiritual force to man and it is to Him that this will return when man dies. Asare Poku (1978) notes that the people of West Africa affirm in their worship that God is a spirit and He is never represented or worshipped through any images. The Ewe also believe in the existence of smaller deities and ancestors, and they acknowledge the existence of bad spirits. This is contrary to Christianity, which does not endorse the worship of gods and ancestors.

The Ewe believe that, as a mark of God's benevolence, they were protected while experiencing many hardships in their migration from

2 According to Greene (2002: 16) and Venkatachalam (2015: 54), the influence of missionary discourse contributed to present attributes of God, while the figure of Mawu — which assumed the characteristics and name of the Christian God — was a rather distant deity in pre-Christian times.

Notsie to their present settlement. The libation prayers to God affirm that without His protection they would have fallen into the hands of the enemy or become prey to the numerous wild animals that they encountered along the way. In Ewe culture, there is an unbroken relationship between the living and the dead; when the material part of a human being dies, the spiritual part continues to live. This means that death does not end life, but rather the dead live in a world close to the world of the living. These worlds are separated by a river that can only be steered by Kutsiami,[3] a boatman who transports the spirits of those who die to the other side of the river where they continue to live and intercede on behalf of those who are living. There is a strong parallel with the river Styx and the ferryman Charon (or Kharon) of Greek mythology, and with the medieval Christian ideas about the afterlife which re-used both Styx and Charon

As indicated by Meyer, "not all dead souls reached or stayed in *tsiefe* [the land of the ancestors]; [...] some spirits of the dead (*ŋɔliwo*) remained on earth to frighten and trouble the living. Those who died prematurely [...] were thought of as continuing to haunt the living. [...] In order to make sure that these *ŋɔliwo* reached *tsiefe*, the living had [...] to perform rites according to the latter's wishes [of the spirits]" (1999: 64).

The people who are living are required to perform rituals so that they can continue to benefit from the spirit world's intercession. First, they have to maintain a healthy environment, which means reconciling all members of the living community by ensuring that they do away with things that will not promote beneficial relationships. They also need to maintain the bond that binds the living and those in the land of the dead. Bad harvest, disease, and misfortune are signs that there is a breakdown of the relationship between the living, the ancestors, and God.

These principles guide the Ewe people in all that they do. They perform rites with drumming, dance to songs composed to praise God, and request the ancestors to continue to intercede on their behalf. They also pour libations to give thanks to both God and the ancestors. Days are set for the observance of these rites. The local people know their

3 This is why a coin is placed in the coffin of the dead to pay Kutsiami for ferrying the soul of the departed to the ancestral world.

roles; they are aware that if they fail to perform these rituals, sanctions will follow. These beliefs regulate the behaviour of the people in their daily lives.

Heritage Material of the Anlo Ewe

While these rituals are also observed by other ethnic groups in parts of Ghana and Togo, my focus in this chapter will be on Anlo heritage rituals observed during fieldwork conducted by Daniela Merolla and myself in the Anlo area in 2007, and our attendance at the Anloga Hogbetsotso festival in 2011. It should be pointed out that a comparison between the Anlo and other Ewe-speaking people shows that many similarities exist between their heritage materials. This could be explained by the fact that these rites were performed and learned by the Ewe in their ancestral settlement before they scattered during migration to their present-day locations (Kodzo-Vordoagu 1994). The Anlo instituted the Hogbetsotso festival in the early 1960s to remember the migration.[4] Similarly, the Asogli[5] people celebrate their festival to remember the part they played in the migration. According to oral sources, they broke the thick wall of Notsie using a sword to facilitate the exodus of the Ewe from Notsie.

Various rituals are an integral part of the festival and are performed to cleanse and reconcile members of the community. They include the following:

1. Dɔɖeɖe: The physical removal of dirt, involving the collection and disposal of unwanted material to the outskirts of the town, beyond the gate-keeper idol that protects the state against spirits that cause deadly diseases in the community.
2. Aƒekpɔkplɔ: The removal of negative metaphysical thought waves, which affect the unity of the state, through mental cleansing.
3. Nugbidodo: The use of water mixed with herbs to sprinkle on people as an act of cleansing and reconciliation.

4 On the history of the Hogbetsotso, see Greene (2002: 26).

5 The Asogli are another Ewe sub-group who migrated from Notsie and settled in Ho, Takla, Kpenoe, and other neighbouring villages in the Volta Region of Ghana. According to oral history, they separated from the Anlo when they reached a place called Tsevie (Klugah 2013: 155).

4. Tsiƒoƒoɖi: A prayer to those members of the community who led exemplary lives before they died, to intercede on on behalf of the present-day group.
5. Abaɖoɖo: A ritual to remember the departed souls of the community by reciting their names and their deeds, and praying to these souls to intercede between the dead and the living. I shall discuss this in more detail later in the chapter.

Drumming and Dancing

Everywhere the Anlo people are found, they come together to organise drumming and dancing as a part of their recreation. According to Ladzekpo (1970), drumming and dancing is a vigorous traditional ensemble art form actively promoted among the Anlo communities through a system of volunteer-run clubs. They appoint their own leaders and work closely under them to compose songs about how they perceive the world and the relationships they engage in. They lampoon these leaders in their songs, to remind them of what befell their despotic chiefs in the past. There are different drumming groups in the communities. This is attested in a series of varied dances, such as war dances, love dances, and recreational dances.[6] The war dance relates to the royal family and those lineages that have roles to play in the royal house. The songs depict martial exploits and the dances portray the greatness of the king. The love songs and dances extol the harmonious relationship between male and female. Other songs address aspects of life including morality, the exercise of authority by rulers, and the socio-economic life of the people. Fiagbedzi (1997) classifies the kinds of music according to song type, drumming type and the instrument used. He notes that there are also leisure-time or boredom-killing dances (*Modzakaɖevuwo*). These dances are performed for entertainment during the harvest time and festivals. Examples of these dances are *Agbadza*, *Woleke*, and *Akpese*.

In storytelling, a member of the audience is permitted to compose a tune for a song that is related to the theme of the story (*Glihawo*). At

6 Examples of such dances are offered in the instructional DVD *Dance-Drumming of the Anlo Ewe featuring the Ghana Dance Ensemble* (Vijay Rakhra Productions 2006).

the beach, when pulling the net in during fishing, people also sing (*Futahawo*). When people are bereaved, they sing to drive away their sorrows (*Avihawo*). People also perform functionally-classified dances for the celebration of their gods, *Trɔvu*, and for war, *Avadevu*.

Ritual dances are reserved for the members of cults. The *Afa* and *Yeve* cults are known to have distinctive dances for when they perform their rites. War dances are performed as a form of recreation to simulate war situations. Examples of these dances are: *Gadzo*, *Atsiagbekɔ*, and *Atrikpui*. On the whole, it can be said that music and dance encompass all aspects of life for the Anlo people.

Sanitation of the Community

Cleanliness is an important aspect in the lives of the Ewe. When the Hogbetsotso festival is approaching, the elders meet to plan a clean-up exercise called Dɔɖeɖe in all of the divisions and towns under the leadership of the chiefs, priests, and elders.[7] The general clean-up starts in August and ends in October. Cleanliness has a spiritual dimension and is treated as such: the people sweep everywhere, including the shrines and the markets,[8] to remove all unwanted materials. They also clear bushes, de-silt drains, and drain stagnant water from gutters. All of these unwanted materials are deposited at the outskirts of the town.

Ewe believe that disease-causing spirits normally seek permission from their gate-keeper idol before entering the community. The permission is granted when the idol realises that the people have left places untidy and have not performed the accompanying rituals. The idol will then allow the disease-carrying spirit to enter the towns and cause sickness. When this fact is brought to the attention of the priests during their routine divine investigation of the state's spiritual position, they act with dispatch to placate the gods. However, when the rituals are performed on schedule, the disease-carrying spirit will spend little time with the gate-keeper idol. It will be turned away and go to other places where people have broken the relationship with their gods. When

7 There are thirty-six Anlo towns. The towns are situated in divisions with their own clan heads, who serve under chiefs.

8 "The purpose is to rid the community of those materials that might contain the ill will that has been brought into the market by Anlo and non-Anlo citizens alike when engaged in the sometimes rancorous business of trade" (Greene 2002: 104).

the waste is deposited at the shrine of the idol in the next village, the people return to their village in silence. A shot is fired at the dumping site and they are forbidden to look back. As Greene writes, the Dɔɖeɖe ritual materialises "the belief in the power of the body through the use of speech", which conforms to older beliefs involving witchcraft, while today "witchcraft accusations are virtually non-existent, replaced by the effort to reconcile those at odds with one another" (2002: 104).

Removal of Negative Thought Waves from the Community

Another important ritual is Aƒekpɔkplɔ, which is mental cleansing involving the use of special herbs. People believe that the state can progress when its people have favourable thoughts, as this will attract positive vibrations. If the king has wronged the people and they hate him, it will result in a situation where both the chief and the people will be ill. A similar belief is reported by Yankah (1999) about the Bono of Techiman in the Brong Ahafo Region of Ghana. He recounts that, in the eighteenth century, the king, Nana Ameyaw, was a tyrant who did not allow the people freedom of expression. This situation resulted in the refusal of support from the region. As a result, he lost the war with the Ashanti and he was captured; upon his release, he committed suicide.

The Bono learnt a lesson from this and agreed to celebrate a festival in which they could criticise their chiefs and elders openly. Agovi (1995), portraying what happened during the Kundum festival of the Nzema people in Ghana, notes that people employ verbal art in the form of songs to lampoon those in authority. He also observes that the poets in the community are so skillful that these songs usually resolve problems with authority.

The mental cleansing of the Anlo people is performed annually, before the Hogbetsotso festival. The assistants of the priest are mandated to go to all of the divisions with a calabash, carrying herbs which have properties for mental cleansing. Anyone who has any grudge against his neighbour is expected to articulate it with a prayer for the success of the state in the presence of the assistant. These verbal requests are believed to be collected alongside a coin that is placed in the calabash. Any person who has a special grievance is permitted to go to the priest and lodge his complaint using this formula. It is believed that all evil thoughts with negative waves will be collected through this method. Such a ritual will be followed with special libation prayers for the cleansing and removal of misfortune from the state.

Libation Prayer

An important ritual that takes place across the whole country, and many parts of West Africa, is Tsiƒoƒoɖi, the libation prayer. It is performed as a part of all the rituals, and it varies according to the occasion. It is a way of thanksgiving and a humble request for protection from God through the intercession of ancestors. *Verba Africana*, vol. 1[9] has documented a libation in a storytelling session for pupils of Seva Zion Primary School. Before starting his story, Kwakuga Goka, the storyteller, poured libation to invite the ancestors to tell a story that would guide the path of the young ones. While he poured the liquor on the ground, he prayed the following:

Tɔgbuiwo, Mamawo
Mia ƒe ahae nye si
Mia va xɔe keŋkeŋ
Alebe susu nava miato gli na ɖeviwo
Woadze fiato adze gato
Ne ɖeviwo
Woazɔ ɖe eŋu estɔ

Ancestors,
This is your drink
I pray that you take all and in return
Grant us knowledge to tell stories
To children in the proper way
To serve as a guide in their life
In the near future

In the formal libation prayer of the Hogbetsotso that we attended in 2011, the priest, Kporvi Nyidewu, accompanied by two assistants, was

9 *Verba Africana*, vol. 1 can be consulted at http://www.hum2.leidenuniv.nl/verba-africana

the celebrant. On such an occasion, the priest steps forward, leaving the two assistants behind. The members of the family are seated and they listen pensively. The priest, holding a calabash containing water mixed with cornflour, calls God and then recites the names and appellations of the ancestors, thanking them for interceding on behalf of the living and protecting the land. He then requests a bumper harvest in the coming year and good health for the people. Occasionally, the two assistants respond in support of the priest to indicate that the humble request he is making is the wish of all assembled. The water mixed with cornflour in the calabash is poured on the ground, followed by liquor. The priest returns to the family and the elders welcome him with special greetings, as if he has returned from a distant land — the world of ancestors and spirits. He responds by saying that he has seen the ancestors and that they accepted the offering and agreed to continue to protect them. Not much is written on this subject, but a few religious leaders think that it should be analysed, in order for us to come to the realisation of the good things in libation and not to consider it sentimentally. Archbishop Akwasi Sarpong supports libation as a form of prayer. However, a number of Christians hold contrary views.[10]

Ensuring the Dead Settle in the Ancestral World

Abaḍoḍo, the laying of the mat ritual, is another important ceremony performed after the death of members of the clan. These rituals are generally performed before Hogbetsotso, which is the first week of November. This is to make sure that the spirits of the dead are properly accepted in the ancestral world before the festival. Clan members assemble at the village courtyard and the elder hands over a ceremonial mat to the chief celebrant. He lays it in the centre of the semi-circle and recites the names and appellations of the departed ancestors. The members of the clan listen pensively, because this is the occasion when they will learn about the lineage of those who have passed on. They will also hear the celebrant's appellations that allude to the important contributions the ancestors made to the community when they were alive.

10 [N.a.], "Don't Downplay Libation at State Functions", *Daily Graphic*, 10 March 2011.

Water is mixed with cornflour in a calabash, and as the celebrant dips his hand in the mixture, the names of the ancestors are called one by one with their appellations. They are humbly requested to accept the mixture with their supplications. The priest prays that the recently departed, whose souls are believed to be transported by the boatman across the river to their world at the other bank, are formally integrated in the world of the ancestors and the water from the pots is poured on the ground as their names are recited again. Liquor is poured, and the celebrant asks the ancestors to continue to intercede on their behalf with God, as well as fight the bad spirits who work against the members of the clan. He also prays for the progress of the state. The celebrant then steps back, and he is welcomed back from his distant journey to the land of the ancestors. This is followed by the serving of drinks to all of the people present. Next, while the royal war drum *Atrikpui* is played, dances around the empty pots of water are performed. This is accompanied by the firing of muskets. Nutsuakor (1977) notes that after all of this, people engage in conversation about social issues and the youth who have reached marriageable age are encouraged to marry in the family.

Reconciliation of the People in the Anlo State

One of the most important traditions is Nugbuidodo. This ceremony is meant to bring peace among the people of Anlo. It takes place on the Thursday before the festival. On this day, all the people of Anloga, the capital city, assemble at Agɔwoʋɔnu, the house where the performance will take place. Here, Togbui Wenya, on arrival at Anloga, performs the ceremony of establishing a settlement (Kodzo-Vordoagu 1994). This place is believed to be the abode of the gods and ancestors. The *Awomefia*, King of Anlo, and his elders first go to the house of *Awadada*, the Field Marshall, to verify that none of the accoutrements that will be used for the ceremony have been tampered with. This is to ensure that these artefacts are spiritually intact. The *Awomefia* leads a procession with special songs to all of the divinities known in the town, announcing his presence to make them formally aware of the reconciliation ceremony.[11]

11 All the important 'gods', are referred to here as divinities. They have their symbols surrounding the outer perimeter of Agɔwoʋɔnu. The procession is led by the Chief to announce the presence of the group to the gods before entering Agɔwoʋɔnu.

When he is satisfied that this is done, he enters the house and takes his ceremonial seat, followed by the Field Marshall, the Chiefs, Priests, Elders and a cross section of the people present. The king's linguist and diplomat is usually the Master of Ceremonies on occasions like this.

The traditional poet and speech mediator announces that all is ready for the ceremony to start, and the *Awomefia* begins to make his address to the people. He ostensibly complains about what happened in the year under review. The address is directed to the following people: the Field Marshall, the Chiefs of the Right, Left and Central wings, the people, and those in charge of the herb. The herb is incorporated into all of the sections of the speech because the herb is believed to have the capacity to remove the ill-feelings that will pour out from the address, ridding the state of the negative thought waves that will harm it.

The king, conscious that he is in the presence not only of the people but also of the gods and the ancestors who are omniscient, solemnly pours out his grievances. An extract from his speech is presented below:

Sɔhɛawo siwo nye Aŋlɔ ƒe adzagba kple sika
Womá womele ɖeka o
Emawo hã nye vevesese le dzi me nam,
Egbe nesee wòage ɖe amatsia me
Đekawɔwɔ neva Aŋlɔ me, miawɔ ɖeka.
Zikpui siwo katã le tenyea,
Wosu gbɔ gake fia mele geɖe dzi o
Mi efiawo mie nutefe wɔm abe alesi
Mia tɔgbuiwo wɔe hegblẽ ɖe anyi na mi ene o.
Mele hadzi ge ade Avadada, aga dzi ade Đusifia kple Miafia ha.
Ne mele wo dim be makpɔ la, nyemele wo kpɔm edziedzi o
Wome kpekpem ɖe ŋunye abe alesi dze ene o
Ema hã nye tamebubu blibo nam be fiawo mesɔ gbɔ ƒo xlãm o.
Đekawɔwɔ neva Aŋlɔ me, miawɔ ɖeka.
Zikpui siwo katã le tenyea, wosu gbɔ gake fia mele geɖe dzi o
Ema hã nye vevesese nam, eya hã neyi ɖe amatsia me.
Đekamawɔmawɔ le Aŋlɔ dukɔa me ya gavem wu nuwo katã
Eye mele edom ɖe ame sia me gbɔ be nye taɖodzinue nye
Be miawɔ ɖeka, mianɔ ɖeka
Aŋlɔdua miagbugbɔ miafɔe ɖe tsitre.
Aŋlɔdua mieva zu kokoe na du bubuwo.
Emawoe nye nye vevesesewo.
Ne emae nye nua, ke nege ɖe amatsia me.

A translation of this extract is as follows:[12]

> The youth who are the precious jewels
> For the adornment of the Anlo state
> Cannot act as one; they are divided
> These are heavy burdens on my heart
> Those in charge of the herb should hear
> Let it go into the herb.
> The stools under me are many
> But only a few of them have chiefs occupying them.
> You, the chiefs are not following the standard
> Set up by our ancestors in the performance of your duties.
> I am pointing the same accusing finger at you,
> The Field Marshall, the Right wing and the Left wing.
> I do not have you supporting me at all times as expected.
> I am extremely worried
> There is widespread disunity in the Anlo state.
> I want to make a passionate appeal to all
> It is necessary for us to unite as one body.
> Other communities now ridicule us.
> These things are actually disturbing my soul.
> If that is the cause of the ill feeling among us,
> Then let it go into the herb.

As the king concludes his presentation, it is believed that the negative thought waves will have found their way into the herbs. The chief's diplomat announces that the priests should note that the king has made an allusive statement against all three of the wings, and summarises what he said by explaining the proverbs.

The Field Marshall then takes his turn to present his side of the case, pointing out what needs to be done in order to obtain unity in the state. The opportunity is given to the wing chiefs to respond to the allegations and the people point out all of the omissions on the part of the rulers. In 2011, a section of the speech of Mr. Yevu Dzeklo, a spokesperson in Ewe, was as follows:

12 I am grateful to Rev. Edem Dande for the translation of the verbal interactions at the 2011 Nugbuidodo ceremony.

Miafe Awɔmefia dze agbagba gake
Nu ɖeka si ke mededem le miagbɔ o,
Ẽ enya wɔ koa ke egblê mi ɖi adzo ayi ablotsi.
Enye mi sɔheɛawo fe didi be alesi mianɔviawo
Dzo le mia domii alebe womegali o,
Gake dzɔgbevɔetɔe wogblê ame aɖewo ɖe megbe
Abe wo viwo ene kple wo srɔwo.
Adze abe, ametsitsiwo gblɔna
Le Aŋlɔ me be 'etɔ kua vie dã'.
Alebe mieva kpɔkpɔm be ɖeviawo va le dadãm.
Koa mienɔ mɔ kpɔm be miafe fiagãwo-
Domefia kple Ɖusifia woale mi afo fu miabu tame aɖe
Tso ameyinugbeawo ŋu, vevietɔe nye
Nu siwo wogblê ɖe megbe
Abe wo viwo kple wo srɔwo ene.
Alebe nu mawo katã nye helehele aɖe tsi akɔta na mi
Alebe miele veve sem tso nuwɔna siawo ŋu.
Ne nu mawo nye nua egbea
Mienɔ anyi ɖe afii le nugbui dom
Egbe nase woayi ɖe amatsia me.

Our king has done well but there is one thing
We are not pleased with:
His frequent visits abroad without prior notice to his council
Is not helpful to the development of the state
There was a disturbance in the state
And some people lost their lives
We have seen that the children
Of these departed souls
Are really suffering
However, nothing was done
To support them.
The youths think that their efforts
Have not been recognised
And rewarded appropriately.
If these are the causes
Of the indiscipline in the state,
As we sit here today
For this reconciliation rite,
Let the herb hear it and put an end to it.

Those in charge of the herbs turn them, mixing the leaves and sprinkling water on them, and they firmly believe that all of the evil thoughts and deeds which came from the king, the elders and the people will go into the herbs, and thus they can move forward, united as one people. In 2011, as they mixed the herb, Mr. Aʋlavi Besa, the Chief Priest for the occasion, uttered the following words repeatedly:

E e egbea, egbee nenye le gbeƒe
Mieva do wò gba,
Etrɔ zu ŋugbi miedo gba,
Miedo ŋugbuia na Awɔmefia, eduawo, efiawo nanye ama kekeke
Oo! Ameʋɔwo tɔe yi! Ameʋɔwo tɔe yi! Miatɔe nye fie.
Efiaa, fiagbe wòdona, Egbea mie gbe do ge, miekpɔ Awɔmefia.
Mie gbe do ge, mie dom ɖe ku dzi o, miedom ɖe ahe dzi o.
Ɖagbe, ɖagbe, ɖagbe, akoe ɖagbe, asi ɖagbe, evi ɖagbe, ketɔ neku hee.
Eye ame yi ke be Awɔmefia meganɔ ne yeanɔ o ɖe,
Nedze ŋgɔ, neyi nɔƒea, neyi nɔƒea wòavae nɔ anyi.
Egbe ya mie dodom fia hã,
Efiawo nesɔ, edu ta bleatɔ vɔ adêa miawo nu nesɔ.

Yes, today you're a plant in the forest,
We plant you today,
You have become a reconciliation herb we plant today,
We plant this herb for the king,
The chiefs and the entire community.
Oh! This is for the enemies! This is for the enemies.
Ours is the evening. A chief should speak like a chief.
Today we plant this herb because we have got a king.
As we plant this herb we do it not for death and not for poverty.
We want blessings in terms of money,
Commercial activity, children; the enemy should die.
Anyone who wishes evil for the king
Should take the lead and dwell in the other world.
The herb that we plant today, the chiefs should be united
All the thirty-six towns should be united.

Water is poured onto the herbs. Then comes the moment when it is splashed on one another, starting with the Awomefia and the wing chiefs. Then it is the present community members' turn. Afterwards, this herbal mixture is collected into fifteen pots for the fifteen clans of Anlo state. The clan elders take charge of these pots to give this sanctified water to their members, according to their need.

The elders point out that the breakup of order in Anlo resulted in the inability of the people to come together and contribute payment for the ram that was used for the reconciliation rites. Everything was left in the hands of a small group and their leaders, whereas it is actually the collective responsibility of all in the state. The ram is slaughtered for communal feasting on that day. Finally, all is set for the people to disperse. The *Awomefia* take the lead and, with songs of joy, move out of Agɔwoʋɔnu. They leave the place in the same order as they arrived. The people return to their homes to prepare for the grand durbar which is taking place the next day. This occasion calls for people to dress in their traditional garb, and it is attended by people from all walks of life. This includes a political figure, to assure the people that they will have their fair share of development projects in the country.

Preservation of Heritage Material

These preparations are done for the Hogbetsotso festival because of the people's conviction that they enable them to forge ahead to develop the area in unity and good health. What clearly stands out is the sanitation ritual, which embodies the general cleanliness of the community and the repair of social cohesion. In addition, there are the democratic ideals of the consultation of the masses before decisions are taken, the submission of the king to the people when he is questioned in public, and the sharing of thoughts and feelings with the whole community. These are very commendable principles which are upheld for the healthy development of any social group.

Expressions of gratitude to God and the ancestors are not left out of the rituals; they are often expressed in the libation prayer. Calling out the names of the ancestors and their achievements preserves them for posterity. While most people do not appreciate the value of the rituals because they have not considered them critically, almost all of the ethnic groups in Ghana use libation as a form of prayer, with very little differences in the actual performance.

Libation was carried out during public performances and state functions (Greene 2002: 80; Coe 2005: 88–89), in addition to Christian and Muslim prayers. Realising the importance of this traditional way of expressing gratitude to God through our ancestors, Okyeame Akuffo was made a State Linguist (speech mediator and poet) by President Nkrumah in the early 1960s.[13] He poured libation with zeal and exceptional oratory, praising God, praying to Him and reciting the names of the ancestors in Akan.

Libation is no longer performed at state functions, and sadly there is an informal[14] debate as to whether it should be continued at all. It would appear that those in authority are more sympathetic to Charismatic Christian arguments against the pouring of libation; many people who oppose it feel the mention of deities and ancestral spirits is demonic. While some agree with this and believe that libations should be left out of state functions, others think the names of the ancestors should continue to be recited because the great things their forbears did are a model for the youth. The traditionalists also maintain that many people do not know their family line beyond their proximate generations, partly because of the absence of some of these rituals. Because of this, people are easily misinformed about the Ewe beliefs and their culture, ending their discussions with erroneous conclusions.[15]

Interviews with teachers, school children, and elders in Accra, Anloga, and in the surrounding areas about their knowledge of the festival and the rituals that are performed before it begins were quite revealing.[16] A majority of the people confessed that all they knew was the drumming, the dancing, and the durbar of the chiefs. Members of the Christian Charismatic faith declared that these rituals should be left to "non-believers", because a Christian should not promote

13 Coe (2005: 88). Okyeame Akuffo was a Research Fellow of the Department of Linguistics, University of Ghana.

14 See Nehusi (2013); Sarpong (1996); Opoku (1978) for arguments for and against libation prayer. The most impressive are the arguments advanced by Archbishop Akwasi Sarpong in support of libation prayer at national functions in Ghana. He notes in his words that libation is a national heritage that could hardly be discarded. He also points out that the absence of libation at national functions could have serious spiritual repercussions on the nation.

15 On the demonisation of local practices see Meyer (1999).

16 In 2006, Daniela Merolla and I conducted these interviews and collected oral narratives at Seva in Southeastern Ghana.

anything that is designed to communicate directly or indirectly with deities and idols. A first result of the interviews was the production of two volumes belonging to the *Verba Africana Series*[17] with the aim to document Ewe cultural heritage and present it with scientifically informed materials and articles addressing various publics. Thanks to the technological opportunities, non-linear hypertexts offer short pieces of information, videos, and sounds for the average reader, while an interested audience with specialized knowledge can access multiple levels of detail through additional hyperlinks. Documentation is necessary to protect vital aspects of this rich cultural heritage from being lost. At the moment, some of the rituals are almost extinct.

As indicated above, the emergence of the Christian Charismatic movement in the country, and the misrepresentation of facts about heritage materials, are posing a great challenge to researchers working on them. These groups are intolerant and vocal antagonists of rituals and practices as they present them as aspects of idol worship. A small group of people is given access to record the rituals, but they do not have the capacity to archive them and they are not able to spread awareness of the educational value that these materials possess. A simple search on the internet shows that dozens of recordings of the Hogbetsotso festival, as well as marriage rites, naming celebrations, and religious songs, are available on YouTube, Facebook, and Ghanaian local and national websites. Unfortunately, recording cultural heritage is not sufficient. As indicated by Merolla:

> [A]udio-video recording has [...] become a fundamental tool for studying oral performances and documenting them for future generations. At the same time, video documentation is not the "ultimate solution" since it only covers a part of the performance; as is the case with written transcription, it implies a process of selection and thus contains the risk of manipulation. Audio-visual recording technology is not only a mechanical tool to record events; it affects what is documented. (2012: 156)

17 http://www.hum2.leidenuniv.nl/verba-africana, vol. 1, *Ewe Stories and Storytellers from Ghana* and vol. 4, *Hogbetsotso: Celebration and Songs of the Ewe Migration Story. Interview with Dr. Datey-Kumodzie.*

People in the area possess a captivating heritage which can only be understood when their discourse and symbolic forms are discussed under the guidance of someone who has the appropriate knowledge of what they represent. Those who condemn these rituals are not fortunate enough to have anyone to account for their value. I therefore suggest organising a forum for people who ascribe value to the culture and aspire for its promotion. The initiation of discussion on how to organise a "Heritage week" in the Ewe communities for both locals and tourists would be of great help. During such a week, the importance of these practices could be supported by providing excerpts of performances, explications in the form of short theatre pieces and lectures, and question-answer meetings with pupils, students and the general public. Moreover, participants in the forum and the Heritage week could pressure school authorities to add topics to the curriculum that would give those who pass through the school system knowledge of the rituals and why they are performed. This would make the country's youth appreciate African festivals, beliefs and rituals. Finally, I suggest that the skills of museum staff be enhanced through in-service training so that they can assist with this project. Inspiration could be taken from the Cultural Bank projects in Mali, Benin, and Togo, which offer "rural populations an opportunity to place their valuable cultural objects in a village museum rather than selling them. In exchange, the villagers are offered financial loans and management training" (Mew 2008).[18] A rebranding and packaging of heritage materials should be worked out by those engaged in the training of the personnel. When the museum staff is trained the service that it will be capable of providing will be highly valued by people in the country, including students and, most importantly, tourists who want to learn about the community's heritage.

18 The Cultural Banks obtained the Culture for Peace Prize by the Chicar Foundation in 2015. See the project description at http://www.fondationchirac.eu/en/conflicts-prevention/the-prize-for-conflict-prevention/the-laureates-in-2015/cultural-banks-of-mali-2015-laureates-for-the-culture-for-peace-prize

References

[N.a.] "Don't Downplay Libation at State Functions", *Daily Graphic*, 10 March 2011.

Agovi, K. (1995) "The King is not Above Insult: The Politics of Good Governance in Nzema *Avudwene* Festival Songs", in: Furnis, G. and Gunner, L. (eds.) *Power, Marginality and African Oral Literature* (Cambridge, Cambridge University Press): 50–73.

Amenumey, D. E. K. (1997) "A Brief History", in: Agbodeka, F. (ed.) *Eweland. The Ewes of Southeastern Ghana*, vol. 1 (Accra, Woeli Publishing Services): 14–27.

Asare Poku, K. (1978) *West African Traditional Religion* (Singapore, FEP International Ltd.).

Coe, C. (2005) *Dilemmas of Culture in African Schools: Youth, Nationalism, and the Transformation of Knowledge* (Chicago, The University of Chicago Press).

Fiagbedzi, N. (1997) "Anlo-Ewe Music and Dance", in: Agbodeka, F. (ed.) *A Handbook of Anlo-Eweland: The Northern Ewes in Ghana* (Accra, Woeli Publishing Services): 153–176.

Gayibor, N. L. and Aguigah, A. (2005) "Early Settlements and Archaeology of the Adja-Tado Cultural Zone", in: Lawrance, B. (ed.) *The Ewe of Togo and Benin* (Accra, Woeli Publishing Services): 1–13.

Greene, S. E. (2002) *Sacred Sites and the Colonial Encounter: A History of Meaning and Memory in Ghana* (Bloomington/Indianapolis, Indiana University Press).

Klugah, M. A. (2013) "Recounting History through Linguistics: A Toponymic Analysis of Asogli Migration Narratives", *African Journal of History and Culture* 5–8: 151–159.

Kobla Ladzekpo, S. and Pantaleoni, H. (1970) "Takada Drumming", *African Music* 4–4 (1970): 6–31.

Kodzo-Vordoagu, J. G. (1994) *Anlo Hogbetsotso Festival* (Accra, Domak Press Ltd.).

Mew, S. (2008) "Public Access to Museums in Ghana and Mali", in: Voogt, P. (ed.) *Can We Make a Difference? Museums, Society and Development in North and South* (Amsterdam, Royal Tropical Institute [KIT]): 98–108.

Meyer, B. (1999) *Translating the Devil: Religion and Modernity among the Ewe in Ghana* (Edinburgh, Edinburgh University Press).

Nehusi, K. (2013) "Libation: A Ritual of Heritage in African Life" http://www.africanholocaust.net/news_ah/libation.html

Nutsuakor, R. K. (1977) *Blema kɔnuwo lododowo kple adaganawo* (Tema, Publishing Division of the Ghana Publishing Corporation).

Opoku, A. K. (1978) *West African Traditional Religion* (Singapore, FEP International)

Sarpong, P. (1996) *Libation* (Accra, Anansesem Publications).

Spieth, J. (2011) *The Ewe People. A Study of the Ewe People in German Togo* (Accra, Sub-Saharan Publishers), http://www.africanbookscollective.com/books/the-ewe-people

Venkatachalam, M. (2015) *Slavery, Memory, and Religion in Southeastern Ghana, c.1850-Present* (London/New York, International African Institute/Cambridge University Press).

Yankah, K. (1999) "Free Speech as Therapeutic Discourse: Ethnography", in: Ameka, F. K. and Cantoments, K. Osam (eds.) *New Directions in Ghanaian Linguistics* (Accra, Black Mask Ltd.): 425–447.

4. YouTube in Academic Teaching: A Multimedia Documentation of Siramori Diabaté's Song "Nanyuman"

Brahima Camara, Graeme Counsel and Jan Jansen

Introduction

This chapter expands the documentation of a video recording of the song "Nanyuman" by Mali's legendary female bard Siramori [Sira Mory] Diabaté (ca. 1925–1989). This unique recording was recently collected in the archives of Radio Télévision Guinéenne (RTG), and was then made available on YouTube. This paper adds a transcription and translation to Siramori's version of "Nanyuman", and this enhancing of the YouTube video is an attempt to produce a teaching tool.[1]

This contribution firstly describes an archival quest in the Guinean sound archives and the unexpected find of a Siramori recording. It then presents a methodological and ethical reflection on the process of archiving and making the recording accessible on YouTube, with further considerations given to academic publications of the recording, thus creating a multimedia supported documentation. Central to this paper is the song text of "Nanyuman", with the text from the example found in the RTG archives presented alongside another interpretation of the same song by Siramori. Thus, the textual dynamics of Siramori's performance are displayed and a clear impression of her artistry is presented.

1 The video is available at https://youtu.be/cb7PAdTryxQ. For the transcription, see page 89.

 https://doi.org/10.11647/OBP.0111.04

Some Unexpected Finds at a Guinean Archive

From 2008–2013, Graeme Counsel undertook an audio project at the Radio Télévision Guinée (RTG) for which he archived, digitized and preserved audio materials from Guinea's Syliphone recording label in addition to audio materials recorded on reel-to-reel magnetic tape.[2] With the death of Guinea's first president Sékou Touré in 1984, Guinea entered a long period of military rule under President Lansané Conté (1984–2008). The revolutionary arts policies of the Touré era (1958–1984), which led to state sponsorship of musicians and orchestras, were abandoned, and the archives, which contained over 10,000 songs, were left in neglect (Counsel 2015). The Conté regime gave scant attention to culture, and less so to reviving memories of Sékou Touré. For several decades, most of the music in the archives was never broadcast on radio or television, and thus the cultural memory of the Touré years was all but erased.

During the project of archiving the thousands of songs on magnetic tape, Counsel commenced researching RTG's video archive, which, although outside the parameters of his project, sat adjacent to the audio archive and contained hundreds of hours of recordings of music. A first find Counsel made was a recording of Kouyaté Sory Kandia (1933–1977), one of Guinea's most acclaimed artists.[3] Dr. Iffono, a former Guinean *Ministère de la Culture, des Arts et Loisirs,* had told him that, when he was minister, he had been searching for the only video recording of Kouyaté Sory Kandia that was believed to exist. The minister informed him that he had in fact traveled overseas to Ghana looking for it, and had considered traveling to Algeria.[4] When Counsel was searching in the RTG's Conakry archives, he discovered a video cassette of Kouyaté Sory Kandia amongst a pile of other videos. The RTG's U-matic video machine was barely working but he asked, unofficially, for a copy of the recording, which he gave to the former minister. One of the reasons for the minister's long and fruitless search is that the Ministry of

2 Graeme Counsel received major research project funding from the British Library's Endangered Archives Programme in 2008, 2009, and 2012–2013. See Counsel (2009, 2012, 2015).

3 The video consists of three songs by Kandia, now available at https://youtu.be/L3RJk1Ld-bU, https://youtu.be/-R0gxpvhosw and https://youtu.be/YSPEuXBGBKM. See also video references below.

4 For material recorded during the *Premier Festival Culturel Panafricain.*

Communication has jurisdiction over the RTG archive, and in Guinea, collaboration and communication between ministries is generally weak.

After finding the Kouyaté Sory Kandia recording, Counsel searched for more videos. His endeavors, however, were brought to a close when the U-matic video machine ceased to function. Nevertheless, through unofficial channels, he had secured several examples of rare and previously unknown videos of Guinean musicians and groups.

The RTG archive appeared to also hold some videos by Malian artists recorded by the Office de Radiodiffusion Télévision du Mali (ORTM). On one of these video cassettes, Counsel noticed Ali Farka Touré's name, and the Siramori track presented in this article is the first track on that video cassette. Since Siramori Diabaté is a Maninka (Malinké) from the town of Kangaba, close to the Guinean frontier, she was popular in both Mali and Guinea, which explains the presence of an ORTM video in the RTG archives.[5]

From Archive to YouTube-Supported Teaching Tool

After archiving and digitizing the video material from the RTG archives, Counsel made it available on YouTube on his Radio Africa channel.[6] Though not part of his archiving project, he deemed the material too important to not share with the wider community. When Counsel completed the archiving project the Guinean government celebrated it through a *soirée* held at La Paillote, a music venue which dates to the early days of Guinean independence. The event was broadcasted live on radio, attended by the minister for Culture, civil servants, and musicians, while the prime minister sent his congratulations. The legendary Les Amazones de Guinée gave a powerful performance,[7] and Radio Africa and its YouTube videos were welcomed as additions to the body of research on Guinean music and culture.

5 To the present day, the practicing musicians in Siramori's family often tour in Guinea. In the 1960s and 1970s, the political elites in both countries highly valued Maninka culture and traditions. See Counsel (2013), (2010); M. Camara (2005); Charry (2000); Skinner (2012). Siramori's call for a better understanding of a woman's position in society, which is one of the main themes of her work (cf. Jansen (1996); Camara (2002); Counsel, Jansen and Camara [accepted for publication]), was of major appeal to both the political regimes of Sékou Touré in Guinea and Modibo Keita in Mali (1960–1968).

6 http://www.youtube.com/user/RadioAfrica1

7 A highlight of this concert can be seen at https://youtu.be/NHIDKJqS57c

At that time, Counsel informed Jansen about the Siramori Diabaté recording available on YouTube, since it is the only known video of one of West Africa's most important artists.[8] Counsel knew about Jansen's ethnographic work on Siramori and her family, the renowned bards ("griots") of Kela (cf. Charry 2000; Simonis 2015), and his efforts to publish text editions of their narratives and songs (Jansen 1996, 2012; *Siramori Diabaté*). Jansen then proposed — not surprisingly, considering his previous work — to publish the text of the Siramori song in order to broaden its audience and contribute to a better appreciation and understanding of the Maninka griots' artistry. The desired result would be a multimedia teaching tool that enhanced the YouTube video with a text edition of the performance. Jansen also proposed that Counsel invite the linguist Brahima Camara, with whom he had previously published song texts by Siramori Diabaté (Camara and Jansen 2013). Counsel accepted. Thus, three authors have contributed to this chapter.

For Counsel, this chapter has come about as a result of the impact of his Radio Africa project. Informing Jansen about the recording was a collegial act, rather than a strategic move to commercialize the recording of "Nanyuman". This chapter seeks to make a strategic statement about the resulting product: a YouTube-supported teaching tool that integrates an artist's lyrics and which is published as a scholarly article.

During the writing process for this teaching tool, it became increasingly apparent that digital archives, and YouTube in particular, pose a great challenge to academics of many disciplinary backgrounds as they seek to have their documents enhanced by transcription and translation, or by other forms of analysis. A YouTube recording, whether it is part of a collection, a (professional) video-clip, or an individual recording, can be a fruitful source for both research and teaching in academic courses on African literature, gender studies, comparative literature, popular culture, oral tradition, history, material culture, etc.

8 There also is a 1985 recording from the Malian national television in which Siramori performs with her cousin Kelabala Diabaté (previously available at https://www.youtube.com/watch?v=pwxvt8qAbj0, the video now appears to have been taken down "due to third-party notifications of copyright infringement"). In Kita in 1985, the regional rival griot families were publicly reconciled, with Kela's griots performing the role of externally appointed negotiators. The event attracted significant media attention in Mali and is the focus of a monograph by Barbara Hoffman 2001. The rivalries among the Kita griots were longstanding, and have served, for instance, as the background for several novels by one of Mali's most acclaimed authors, Massa Makan Diabaté, who is himself a griot of Kita origin.

In particular, when enhanced by a transcription and a translation, we see many opportunities for YouTube recordings in the classroom. We hope that the present text inspires scholars to integrate video recordings from archives and new and social media into their teachings.

At the same time, however, we feel our enthusiasm tempered by concerns of authorship and acknowledgment. We are cognizant of deliberations regarding "standard" situations of collecting oral material and returning it later (digitally) to the creators (see Merolla, this volume: 5; see Shetler, this volume: 23). The situation of the Siramori song, however, is complex. None of the authors may derive claims or rights from having been involved in the original recordings as the song resides within an oral tradition shared by many Mandé performers. Future researchers of African heritage may find themselves in similar positions as we find ourselves *vis-à-vis* Siramori's "Nanyuman". Therefore we amply discuss our deliberations during the preparation of the teaching tool.

Some Methodological and Ethical Reflections

We are indebted to Siramori Diabaté in particular and to the Kela griots in general. We acknowledge their art and profession, while also acknowledging ethical and legal issues at stake. Ethically speaking, issues of transparency and accountancy need clear elaboration. While writing this article, Counsel deliberated whether he should reveal to the RTG staff the source of the video, since they were oblivious to its existence — it being but one video from Mali amongst thousands of others from Guinea. Doing so would reveal how Counsel acquired copies of the videos: not through formal channels, but through informal processes. Many senior Guinean government representatives and artists were cognizant of how Counsel obtained the video, and considered the methods a better option than the former practice of neglecting the nation's unique cultural materials by keeping them hidden from public view for decades, where they slowly disintegrated through a lack of preservation.[9] These government representatives and prominent

9 The audio-visual archives at the RTG have not been well maintained. In addition to over 10,000 audio recordings on ¼" magnetic tape, there are thousands of hours of video recordings covering news items, documentaries, sports, interviews, and music, and several hundred reels of the committee meetings and speeches of Sékou

musicians in Guinea were his moral community and he made the recording freely available for scholarly and research purposes via YouTube, recognizing its value as the only known video of Siramori.

In documenting intangible heritage, such as through this discussion of the video of "Nanyuman", the authors' motivations are borne from the "Nanyuman" video's unique qualities and a desire to share these with the wider community. In pursuance of this, however, there are further ethical issues to consider which are complicated by the process of documenting intangible heritage through digital media. Principal among these are legalities concerning copyright. In the case of Siramori's "Nanyuman" it is impossible to determine whether the composition is traditional[10] or the artist's personal composition/interpretation. In a shared oral tradition such as that of the Maninka griots to which Siramori belongs, where songs are passed from one generation to another with and without the performer's own embellishments, ownership of songs is far from clearly established. Thus, questions such as who holds the copyrights — the performer, her inheritors, the griots from the village of Kela (where Siramori grew up and received her artistic training), the ORTM, YouTube, or a combination of these stakeholders — is a near impossible matter to resolve. It is further complicated as to whether the copyrighted material pertains to the lyrics, the video recording, the performance, or combinations of all three. In this regard, YouTube suggests consulting the advice of an attorney, and while such a process would provide a legal framework that assures the right of the individual,[11]

Touré and the Parti Démocratique de Guinée. The archive constitutes a major repository of materials from the Sékou Touré era, though much was destroyed in the months following Touré's death (for example, the collections of Syli Film and Syli Photo). The RTG has digitized some of the material but it is kept locked in a cupboard and is never broadcast.

10 "Nanyuman" has been recorded by other artists, including l'Orchestre Régional de Kayes, https://nextpreview.soundcloud.com/sterns-music/orchestre-regional-de-kayes

11 The legal framework may emanate from either the country in which the attorney works or the country of the performers. We note that institutions that are supposed to represent local artists barely function and are criticized by indigenous artists as corrupt. See Counsel's reference to "Eating the Money" on his Radio Africa website — http://www.radioafrica.com.au/EAP_2008.html. We doubt, for instance, if the publication of the lyrics of "Nanyuman" is of any concern to the BUMDA, the Bureau Malien du Droit d'Auteur, or to their Guinean counterpart, the Bureau Guinéen des Droits d'Auteur (BGDA) — both do not have a functioning website. The reason for the existence of the BUMDA and the BGDA is, principally, to prevent piracy, which is a significant problem in both Mali and Guinea.

it circumvents the politicized reality of a heritage's multi-layered and often situational ownership, as well as issues of temporality. On the other hand, we foresee the impossibility of casting a representative community as the copyrights' stakeholder.[12]

We are therefore caught between our ideals to preserve and document oral tradition and the temptation to focus on the end product, thus performing an "idealization" of our research and concealing what Goffman refers to as "the dirty work" (Goffman 1990 [1959]: 89). Given that there are no strong local and national organizations or legislatures to claim and protect intangible heritage in Mali and in Guinea, we can present our work as meeting the ideal of documentation through our efforts at saving, translating and teaching "Nanyuman". We acknowledge that our ideals to preserve cultural documents by transferring them through new, access-free media to a wide variety of audiences are inspired by an ideology of "web democracy", which is an ideology of an *alleged* open society that is, in practice, accessible only to an elite, although we are happy to see that this elite is growing fast in number thanks to, on the one hand, the spread of mobile phones worldwide and, on the other hand, to apps like Worldreader's and projects like Open Book Publishers and other Open Access initiatives. We apologize for creating this limited access to Siramori's heritage and, at the same time, we hope that Siramori's artfulness in the format of an academic text will enrich scholarship and research. Further, had Siramori been alive today, we feel that she would either consider this paper as being a respectful account of (her) intangible heritage or would treat us with the same understanding given to her heroine, the runaway Nanyuman, by her first husband.

Siramori Diabaté and "Nanyuman"

Siramori's career is firmly based within the heritage of the famous griots of Kela (Jansen 1996). Born in ca. 1925, she was among the first wave of female artists who conquered Mali and Guinea's male dominated

12 As an illustration of the local tensions regarding intangible heritage in the area where Siramori lived, see the ownership discussion related to the Sunjata epic in Kela (Jansen 2012) and the process through which local stakeholders acquired UNESCO recognition of Mande oral traditions as a Monument of Intangible Heritage (cf. Smith 2010; Simonis 2015).

music scene in the 1970s, a process described in detail by Lucy Durán (2007). As Durán explains, the introduction of the microphone to a large extent led to the emancipation of the female voice. This new technology neutralized the decibel advantage that male voices traditionally had over female voices — a situation that for centuries often limited women to background chorus singers.

Siramori declared that "Nanyuman" is her favorite song (Hale and Sidikou 2012: 147; *Sòròfè* [n.d.], end of Side A). Her interpretations indeed show that she was able to produce entertaining variations, undoubtedly adapted to the audiences she had in mind or was performing for. The interpretation available on YouTube via Radio Africa is a live recording, in which the audience is highly amused by the dialogues between Nanyuman and the traveling kola nut merchant who seduces her.[13]

For comparison, a second interpretation is included here which augments the lyrics in the video recording. This version was performed by Siramori for Mali's national radio, probably in the 1960s or 1970s. In this alternate version she evokes a sorority with the adult women of Mali by emphasizing marital values and elaborating less on the domestic scenes and conversations. Originally, Brahima Camara knew this song as a recording by Radio Mali. He purchased a copy in the 1990s at the central market in Bamako from, what he calls, "un revendeur". As in the YouTube case, it is unclear who has rights over Siramori's performance/ artistic production.

Conclusion

Siramori Diabaté has become one of the best documented female voices of West Africa. The discussion of Siramori's interpretations in *Women's Voices from West Africa* volumes 1 and 2, published by Sidikou and Hale (2012) and Hale and Sidikou (2013), very much illustrates her presence and influence in West Africa.[14] This current text underscores these earlier publications by providing further examples of her artfulness.

---

13 Siramori's interpretation of "Nanyuman" on *Sòròfe* [n.d.] is performed for a live audience and elaborates on the dialogues between Nanyuman and the traveling merchant — the audience is highly amused by it. For a literary and social analysis of the song "Nanyuman", see Counsel, Jansen and Camara (under review).

14 As another illustration of Siramori's present-day status in Mali, two collections of her best songs, collected by Mali's Ministry of Culture, were published as "Musique du Mali I: Banzoumana" (Syllart/Mélodie 38901–2) and "Musique du Mali II: Sira Mory" (Syllart/Mélodie 38902–2).

Issues also raised in this paper concern the authors' position as scholars when using Siramori's song book. We have noted ethical and legal issues, and we contend that the use of Siramori's songbook is inevitable and necessary to explain her artfulness to fellow scholars and students. We signaled a form of appropriation by us, the authors, from which the local artists do not and cannot profit. This painful observation is, it appears, an inevitable fact for researchers who document, preserve and use recordings of oral performances.

Fig. 4.1 Screenshot from the recording of Siramori's "Nanyuman". A transcription of the lyrics is presented below. Watch this performance on YouTube at https://youtu.be/cb7PAdTryxQ

"Nanyuman" by Siramori Diabaté

…[15] *kiri ni wɔyɔ.*
… confusion and discord.

Fufunintiki di n nɛnɛ, Kanja Burema.
Kanja Burema, it's the carrier of the little basket who deceived me.

Aaa, n ko wadi le nɔɔ, Kanja Burema.
Oh! Kanja Burema, it's the carrier.

Aaa! Fufunintiki di n nɛnɛ Kanja Burema.
Kanja Burema, it's the carrier of the little basket who deceived me.

15 The first few seconds of the recording are missing.

Ayiwa n badennu!
Yes, dear audience!

Ne Siramori Jabate kan ye nin di.
It's me, Siramori Diabaté, speaking.

N ye min fɔla nin, n yɛdɛ sɔn lee.
The story I tell here is of my own failings.

N t'a fɔla aw kelen ma dɛ mosolu,
Women! My story is not directed at you alone,

N yɛdɛ sɔn lee.
because it's also of my own failings.

Fɔlɔ ngaralu
The famous griots of the past

Oyi ye nin fɔ fɔlɔ mosoyi ye,
have told this story to the women of their time,

Oyi da fudu bato.
and they remained faithful to their marriages.

Ne fɛnɛ y'a yida.
It's my turn to tell.

Mali mosolu, n y'a yida ayi la dɛ
Women of Mali, it's my turn to tell [it to] you,

Ayi fɛnɛ ka fudu bato.
so that you remain faithful to your marriage.

Nanyuman, fin t'a n'a kɛ tɛ.
Nanyuman had no problem with her husband.

Fɔlɔmɔkɔlu le tun b'a kɛ -
In the past people did as follows -

Nɛkɛsoko tele tɛ, motoko tele tɛ,
when there was no bicycle or moped,

Ka worofufunin ta.
people wore small baskets of kola nuts.

N'ayi da woropanyɛ ta, ayi bɛ dɔ bɔ o dala
When buying a big basket of kola nuts, they put some of them

K'o kɛ fufunin dɔ, k'o l'i kun, ka wa duku ni duku.
in a smaller basket which they carried on their head from village to village.

Fufunintiki nada jiki Kanja Bureme kan.
A carrier of a little basket came to Kanja Burema's home.

A ko Kanja Burema, i tɛ hina n na,
"Kanja Burema!" he said. "Have pity on me,

N kɛ tele fila nin kɛ i fɛ yan.
so I can stay few days here at your home.

N bɛ n yaara bukudabolo ninnu na,
I'm going to walk to the neighbouring villages,

Ka n ya woro yaara.
to sell my kola nuts."

Kanja Burema ko, o tɛ baasi di.
Kanja Burema replied, "That's no problem."

Nanyuman! Dɛbɛn ta i k'a la bolon kɔnɔ.
"Nanyuman!" [he called], "Go and put the sleeping mat on the floor of the entrance hut.[16]

Jula le bɛnni bolon kɔnɔ.
Because a traveling merchant likes an entrance hut."

Nanyuman da bolon fida,
Nanyuman swept inside the entrance hut,

Ka dɛbɛn ta, k'a la fufunintiki nya.
then took a mat and spread it out for the carrier of the little basket.

A tanbeda sakuma, ka wa a ya fɛnnu feere
In the morning, he went to sell his produce

16 *Bolon* = hut with two doors that functions as the entrance of a traditional Maninka compound — in French often translated as *vestibule*. In the region south of Bamako, some prestigious families own a *bolon* as a sanctuary, the most well-known being the Kamabolon in Kangaba.

A nada wura la.
and he returned in the evening.

A talada i kɔ, o dukusagwɛ, ka wa a ya fɛnnu feere
The next day he went again to sell his produce

A nada wura la.
and returned in the evening.

Kanja Burema wad'a ya daba l'i kanna
At the same time, Kanja Burema put his hoe on his shoulder

Ka tanbe ka wa fodo dɔ.
and went to the field.

Nanyuman wilida telekunna dɔ
Nanyuman rose in the early afternoon

Ka wa don fufunintiki kan.
and joined the carrier of a little basket.

Fufunintiki ko, eh Nanyuman!
The carrier of the little basket exclaimed "Eh Nanyuman!

I nalen n badola wa?
Did you come to talk to me?"

Ɔɔhɔ, n nalen i bado la bi sa n fa.
"Yes, sir, finally, I came today to talk with you."

A ko Nanyuman!
"Nanyuman!" he continued,

I tɛ woro dɔ ta!
"Have a kola nut!"

Nanyuman ye woro ta.
Nanyuman took the kola nut.

Ee, mosolu! Lahawutani, walakuwata! An ka siran!
Hey, women! How can this be possible! We should be in fear [of punishment]!

Nanyuman ye woro wo ta, a y'o nyimi.
Nanyuman took the kola nut and chewed it.

A ko: Nanyuman!
He said to her: "Nanyuman!

A ko: e moso nyumanba nin!
You are a very beautiful[17] woman!

A ko: i dɔnɔkɔnya dɔgwɛ kɛ!
But it looks like you are deprived!

Ne natuma ni kelen ni sisan tɛ, jurukenin kelen nin le y'i kanna.
Since I've been here, you've worn only one blouse.

Ne ma juruke gwɛdɛ y'i kanna.
I've not seen you wear another."

A ko: Aaa nfa! Nayi ye an ta lanɔkɔ nin le dɔ yan.
She replied: "Oh, sir! We live in misery here."

A ko: Nanyuman!
"Nanyuman!" he replied.

N'i kɛda ne fɛ,
"If you love me,

Ni sanu don, n b'o d'i ma.
if it is gold, I'll give it to you.

Ni wadi don, n b'o d'i ma,
If it is money, I'll give it to you.

Ni fani n[y]uman don, n b'o d'i ma.
If it is beautiful clothes, I'll give it you."

A ko: Aaa n fa!
"Ah, sir!" replied Nanyuman,

N'i kɛda kɛ n fɛ, n fana y'i fɛ wala.
"If you love me, I love you too."

A ko: Ayiwa Nanyuman!
"Okay!" he continued.

N'i kɛ nada bi, n bɛ n sara ko n bɛ wa so sa.
"When your husband returns from the field, I will say my farewells to him.

17 *Nyuman* means morally good, a concept which should not be mixed with *di*, which means good for taste, smell, touch, weather, etc. (but is never used to describe human beings); a beautiful woman is always *nyuman*. Note that *nyuman* is part of Nanyuman's name (cf. Derive 2008).

Sini sakuma, n bɛ n bolofinnu ta, n bɛ wa.
And I will pick up my things to leave tomorrow morning.

Ayiwa Nanyuman!
So, Nanyuman!

Ayi ya kuruninkun min ye yen,
At the little plateaux, yonder,

N bɛ wa n siki yen, k'i makɔnɔ.
I'll sit and wait for you.

I ka wa n sɔdɔ yen.
You and I will meet there."

A ko: Wa! N y'i kɔ.
"Okay, I will join you", said Nanyuman.

Kɛ wo d'i siki kuruninkun dɔ.
The man went and sat down at the plateaux.

Ee Mosolu!
Oh women!

Nanyuman nada, k'a bolofɛnnu fara nyɔkɔn ma,
Nanyuman picked up her belongings,

K'a ya sokɔnɔla fida, k'a hɛɛn.
swept her room, and took off.

Kɔsɔkɔsɔ kɔsɔkɔsɔ![18]
Zjouf zjouf!

Nanyuman wada o kɛ kɔ.
Nanyuman had run off with the man.
(… [after some time]…)

Ka kɛ wo ya sanu ban,
The man's gold was exhausted,

K'a ya wadi ban.
his money was gone.

18 An idiophone expressing speed.

A ko: Nanyuman! Kabini n d'i fudu, fɛn wo fɛn tɛlɛ n bolo, a bɛɛ banni.
He said: "Nanyuman since I married you, all my wealth has vanished.

N t'i fɛ bi, n t'i fɛ sini, n t'i fɛ sinikɛndɛ.
I don't love you anymore. Not today, tomorrow, or the day after."

Nanyuman! Nanyuman ye duku min dɔ
Nanyuman! He left the village where he lived with Nanyuman

Kɛ d'o duku bila, ka wa duku gwɛdɛ dɔ.
to settle in another village.

O tuma Kanja Burema ko.
Kanja Burema received word.

Ko ne ni n moso ma kɛlɛ,
"I did not quarrel with my wife,

Fin tɛ an ni nyɔkɔn tɛ, gwɛ tɛ an tɛ.
so there is no problem between us.

Ne moso wo ka tunun, ne t'o nyini abada.
If my wife vanished under those conditions, I'll never find her.

Ala bɛ wa nyini k'o di ne ma.
But God will go searching for me and bring her back."
[after some time]

Nanyuman wada ole dɔ
Nanyuman went

K'i sɛnsɛn wuruu, ka na se so.
slowly to the village, to reach home.

A nad'a fa sɔdɔ
She went to her father

A ko: Aaa n buwa! I d'a fɔ n yé dɛ!
and said: "Oh daddy! You had warned me well!

O kɛ n'i ban ne dɔ.
The man has left me.

Hali ne ye duku min dɔ, k'o bɛɛ bila ka wa duku gwɛdɛ dɔ.
He even left the village where we lived to go to another village."

A ko: Aaa n den! N y'a fɔ i ye di?
The father replied: "Ah, my daughter! What did I say?"

A ko Nanyuman! I kɛlanka kɔdɔyi ya sanba nalen
"Nanyuman", he continued, "the family of your former husband has sent a message

K'i denkɛnin kelen najikitɔ. O ko ye di?
that your only son will soon be circumcised. What is your situation?"

A ko: Aaa n buwa! O ko tɛ nya gwɛdɛ ma.
"Oh father! It must go ahead.

Ayi bɛ jenbefɔlayi nyini,
Search for the jembe players,

Ka balafɔlayi nyini,
search for the balafon players,

Ka jalimosongarayi nyini.
search for the best female griots.

N ka la ayi kan
I will join them to

Ka wa n den soli si n kɛ kɔdɔ bada,
go and celebrate with my ex-husband the circumcision ceremonies of my son,

N kɛ ka samada kɔdɔ ta, ka n jufidi mabɛnbɛn.
and to allow my husband to spank my bottom with an old shoe."

Ayiwa, n badennu! Nanyuman dontɔ,
So, dear audience! Nanyuman,

Kɛ kuda bid'i b'an dɔ,
after her new husband had abandoned her,

A kɛ kɔdɔ, a dontɔ o bada, a ye dɔnkili min la.
returned home to her former husband and sang a song.

N k'o la wa?
Shall I sing it for you?
[the rest of the song is in song mode]

A ko Nanyuman d'i ban a kɛ fɔlɔ le dɔ
Nanyuman abandoned her first husband

A d'i bari kɛkudalu fɛ, kɛkudalu d'i ban ne dɔ.
to escape with a new one that left her in turn.

Aaa kɛkɔdɔlu kɔnɔnyafɔlɔ lajikitɔ, dimi ma to baasi dɔ.
Ah, the first born of the former husband will be circumcised,
patience can meet any challenge.

Tan-tɛ-n-kɔnɔ, n'a bɛ kɛla tan
I did not expect this, but if everyone was treated that way

Dinya d'i fɛrɛ dɔɔnin.
life would be more peaceful.

Ayiwa n'a bɛ kɛla jonjonjonyi na tan wo, an di fɛrɛ dɔɔnin.
If everyone who ran away was treated that way, life would be more peaceful.

Aaa n'a bɛ kɛla tan
Ah, if everyone was treated that way

Dinya ye suma dɔɔnin.
life would be more peaceful.

N'a bɛ kɛla kɛdabanmosoyi la tan wo, ɔdi fɛrɛ dɔɔnin.
If all women who leave their husbands were treated that way, life would be more peaceful.

Kanja Burema lee, n'a bɛ kɛla tan
Kanja Burema, if everyone was treated that way

Dinya di fɛrɛ dɔɔnin.
life would be more peaceful.

Ayiwa n'a bɛ kɛla minantalayi la tan wo, an di fɛrɛ dɔɔnin.
If all those who are packing their bags were treated that way, we would be more peaceful.

Aaa, n'a bɛ kɛla tan
Ah, if everyone was treated that way

Dinya ye suma dɔɔnin.
life would be more peaceful.

N'a bɛ kɛla kɛdabanmosoyi la tan wo,
If all women who leave their husbands were treated that way,

Dinya di fɛrɛ dɔɔnin.
life would be more peaceful.

"Nanyuman" by Siramori Diabaté[19]

Iyo, Kanja Burema le!
Yes, Kanja Burema!

Ko wadi le nɔɔ.
It is the fault of money.

Ah! N ko wadi ni wɔyɔ!
Oh! Money sows discord!

I m'a ye faransewadi di n nɛnɛ.
You see, French money deceived me.

A ko Nanyumanin le Nanyumanin le!
Little Nanyuman! Little Nanyuman!

Se bɛ moso min ye bɛɛ ye fudu mara.
A woman who can should take care[20] of her marriage.

Hali se tɛ moso min ye bɛɛ fudu, i kana niminsa.
Even a woman who can't, should take care of her marriage, or she will later regret it.

Mosoninmɛsɛnnu le, bɛɛ ye fudu mara, i kana niminsa.
Young women! You should take care of your marriage, or you will later regret it.

Moso karankɛlalu le, bɛɛ ka fudu mara, i kana niminsa.
Educated women! You should take care of your marriage, or you will later regret it.

Ah! Ah! Mosofudukɛlalu le, bɛɛ ye fudu mara, i kana niminsa.
Ah! Ah! Married women! You should take care of your marriage, or you will later regret it.

Mosotɔkɔmalalu le, bɛɛ ye fudu mara, i kana niminsa.
Pregnant women! You should take care of your marriage, or you will later regret it.

---

19 This transcription and translation has been based on a commercial cassette that was available to Brahima Camara in 2000, when Jan Jansen stayed with his family. At this very moment we don't know of any available copy of this recording.

20 *Mara* = to guard.

Dɔnkililajelu le n'ayi ma fudu mara, ayi bɛ niminsa.
Female singers, if you don't take care of your marriage, you will later regret it.

Eh! Eh! Bɛɛ ka fudu mara, i kana niminsa.
Eh! Eh! Everyone should take care of their marriage, or they will later regret it.

Malimosoninmɛsɛnnu le bɛɛ ka fudu mara, i kana niminsa.
All young women of Mali should take care of their marriage, or they will later regret it.

Soloyo, n bɛ sinbon mawelela, Madujinba ni Farajinba.
Soloyo! I call to commemorate the brave Madu Jinba and Faran Jinba.

Aa, aa, Ala tɛ lɔn.
Ah! Ah! No one knows God [well enough].

Jɔn kana baka jɔnnɔkɔon na.
No slave[21] should insult another slave.

Ayi m'a ye jɔn bɛɛ n'i lakunu kan.
See that every slave has his destiny.

A ko Nanyumanin le, Nanyuman le!
Little Nanyuman, little Nanyuman!

Ah Ne baden silamalu ayi ni ke!
Ah! Dear audience,[22] I greet you!

Ne Siramori Jabate natɔ yɔrɔnin min fɔla nin di.
I, Siramori Diabaté, I have come to tell you something.

Hadama, n'i ka dɔnkili wo dɔnkili la, ni kɔdɔ t'a la,
If someone sings a song that doesn't make sense,

A bɛ mɔkɔyi kɔnɔdɔfili.
it will confuse the people.

A kɛkun le fɛlɛ ne fɛ nin di, k'a kɔdɔ l'a kan ayo k'a mɛn — Nanyuman.
For this reason I will sing you a song, and clarify its meaning — Nanyuman.

21 We read "slave" here as a "servant of God".

22 *baden* = kinship term that expresses harmony, literally "children of the same father and the same mother; *silimalu* (pl.) = (lit.) "Muslim", but usually used to address a group of people in a respectful way.

Hali ne yɛdɛ min kan y'a lala nin di, ne Siramori Jabate, n ye moso di.
I myself, Siramori Diabaté, whose voice sings this, I am a woman, too.

Mosolu, ayi ye hakɛto dɛ,
Women, I apologize,

Ne yɛdɛ kan y'a lala; n yɛdɛ sɔn y'a di.
[because] what my own voice sings is about my own failings.

Nk'a fɔlen mosolu ye, oyi y'i miiri a kuma ma, fɔlɔ ngaralu fɛ, ka furu bato.
But it was told by the famous griots of the past, for the women who contemplated about these words, in order to remain faithful to their marriages.

N kɛkun ye k'a fɔ alu ye ole di.
For this reason I sing you this song.

Malimosolu, ayi wo ne wo, an bɛɛ k'an miiri kuma nin ma, an ka fudu bato.
Women of Mali! You and I should contemplate about these words, in order to remain faithful to our marriages.

Nanyuman y'a kɛ kan, kɛlɛ t'a n'a kɛ tɛ.
Nanyuman lived in harmony with her husband.

Fufunintiki dɔ nalen.
There (once) came a carrier of a small basket.

I komi n y'a fɔ alu ye nya min ma, fɔlɔmɔkɔlu tun bɛ woro kɛ worosakinin dɔ, k'a lasidi,
As I have told you, in the past people packed kola nuts in little hives,

K'a l'i kun, k'i tɔkɔma duku nin duku tɛ k'a yaara.
And carried these on their heads from village to village [to sell them].

Worofufunintiki, a nada se Nanyuman kɛ ma.
A carrier of a little basket of kola nuts came to Nanyuman's husband.

Ko Kanja Burema, I tɛ hakɛto n ka bi ni sini f'I fɛ, ka n ya woro mayida dɔɔni.
He said: "Kanja Burema, please allow me to stay at your place today and tomorrow, to sell my kola nuts in the area.

N bɛdɛ n tɔkɔma yɔrɔlu fɛ, n bɛ se ka na si fɛ yan.
When I go from place to place during daytime, I can pass the night here at your place."

O ko o moso ma ko Nanyuman,
He [Kanja Burema] called his wife: "Nanyuman,

K'i bɛ bolonkɔnɔla fida, i ka wa dɛbɛn dɔlu bila yen.
sweep the interior of the entrance hut, and put there some sleeping mats.

Ko bawo k'olu ye julalu di, k'ayi bɛnnin bolon ne kɔnɔ.
Because this man is a traveling merchant, and these [merchants] feel better in an entrance hut."

O ye bolon fida,
She swept the entrance hut,

Ka lolankɛ rɔbɛn, a n'a bolofɛnnu, ka w'a bila yen.
and prepared it for the guest — his belongings were deposited there.

Aa, aa, Nanyuman!
Ah! Ah! Nanyuman!

A ye su fula kɛ, a b'i miiri.
For two nights he [the guest] contemplated.

N'a ye fɛn o fɛn fɔ, Nanyuman b'o bɛɛ d'a ma.
Nanyuman gave him everything that he asked for.

A su filanan dukusɛgwɛlen,
After the second night, a new day started,

Telekunna dɔ, kɛ bada wa konko dɔ.
In the early afternoon, the husband went to his field.

A walen konko dɔ, Nanyuman ye kodo ta,
After he had gone to his field, Nanyuman took a stool,

A nada don kɛ fɛ bolon na, k'i sik'a fɛ.
And seated herself next to him [the guest] in the entrance hut.

Lolankɛ ko Nanyuman, k'e tɛ woro fɛ wa?
"Do you like kola nuts?" the guest asked to Nanyuman.

Ko n ye woro fɛ kɛ.
"I really like kola nuts."

K'i tɛ dɔ ta!
"Then take some."

Nanyuman ye woro dɔ ta.
Nanyuman took a kola nut.

Lolankɛ ko ee, Nanyuman, ko kelen yɛdɛ nɔ ye ne bali:
The guest said: "Nanyuman, I am surprised about one thing:

Ne tele fila ye yan ayi bada ni.
I have lived here at your place for two days.

Ne nya y'i la, i mafani nɔkɔlen, i nyama nɔkɔlen.
I see you look poor and wear only this dirty cloth.

Nin moso nyumanba nin!
A very beautiful woman like you!

E k'i kɛnya dɔgwɛ sa kɛ!
Look how you look like!

N'i di ne sɔn ne dɔ, walahi Nanyuman, n b'i fudu.
I swear [by God], Nanyuman, when you love me, I will marry you.

N b'i fudu, n bɛ fani d'i ma, n bɛ wadi d'i ma, n bɛ sani d'i ma.
I will marry you, give you clothes, give you money, give you gold."

Nanyuman ko: Aa, nfa, nayi ye an ta nyadɔban nin le dɔ yan.
Nanyuman said: "Ah, sir! We live here in misery.

N'i kɛdɛkɛ n fɛ, n fɛnɛ y'i fɛ wala.
If you love me, I will love you the same.

Tɔ tɛ n na.
I can't stand it anymore."

Lolankɛ ko: Nanyuman, sini n bɛ n sara i kɛ la ko n wato.
The guest said: "Tomorrow I will say goodbye to your husband.

N bada wa, n bɛ wa i makɔnɔn dukusokɔfɛ, fukaninkun na.
But I will wait for you behind the village, in the open space in the bush."

O dukusagwɛlen, lolankɛ d'i sara Nanyuman kɛ la, a wada.
On that day the guest said goodbye to Nanyuman's husband, and he departed.

Nanyuman y'i lɔ a kɛ ka wa fodo dɔ.
Nanyuman waited until her husband went to his field.

O walen, a d'a ya minannu daladɛ; a d'a kɛ hɛɛn.
After he had left for his field, she took her belongings, and fled.

Kanja Burema nada ka bɔ konko dɔ.
Kanja Burema returned from his field.

A ko Nanyuman bɛ min? Ee, n moso ka tunun kun t'i la.
"Where is Nanyuman?" he asked, "has my wife disappeared without a reason?

N t'o nyini, Alla b'o nyini!
I won't track her down, but God will!"

A wada kɛ wo fɛ.
She departed with this man.

Wadi banda, sani banda.
(…[after some time]…)
His money finished, his gold finished.

Ko Nanyuman ma n t'i fɛ bi n t'i fɛ sini.
He said to Nanyuman: "I don't love you anymore.

Kabini n d'i fudu, n na wadi bannin n na sani bannin.
Since I married you my money is finished, my gold is finished."

Ayi ye duku min dɔ, a y'o bila Nanyuman kɔsɔn, ka wa duku gwɛdɛ dɔ.
Because of Nanyuman he left his village and he settled in another village.

Nanyuman sakeda ka n'a fa la lu ma.
Nanyuman returned to her father's compound.

A ko aa, aa, n fa, i nɔ ye a fɔ n ye, ko n kana wa kɛ nin fɛ.
"Aa, aa, daddy", she said, "you advised me not to accompany this man.

I nɔ ye a fɔ min ma a kɛlen tan.
Things have happened as you said.

A fɛlɛ nin di a nɔ ye i ban n dɔ.
Now he has abandoned me."

A fa ko, ko sanba nalen ka bɔ i kɛlakɔrɔ dɔ, k'i denkɛninfɔlɔ lajikitɔ sini.
Her father said: "The old husband has informed us that your first son will be circumcised tomorrow."

Nanyuman ko, fo ni n sakeda n kɔ ka na n den soli si,
Nanyuman said: "I have to return to my husband in order to celebrate the circumcision,

N kɛ ka samadakɔdɔ ta ka n jufidi mabɛnbɛn.
And to let my husband spank my bottom with an old shoe."

O kɛlen o dɔ: o da jenbetikilu nyini, ka jalimosongaralu nyini, k'olu bil'a kɔ ka taka.
And so it happened: she assembled djembe players and griottes, to accompany her.

Ee, ee, mosolu, Nanyuman ye dɔkili min la a kɛlasokɔfɛ a n'a ya fɔlilayi dontɔ a kɛkɔdɔ bɛdɛ, n b'o yɔrɔ fɔ ayi ye. A ko:
Women! I will sing for you the song by Nanyuman and the musicians at the entrance of the compound of her old husband. It says:
[the following is in song mode]

Nanyuman d'i ban a kɛfɔlɔ le dɔ, a d'i bari kɛkudalu fɛ.
Nanyuman abandoned her first husband and settled with a new one.

Aa, kɛkudalu d'i ban ale dɔ.
But the new one abandoned her.

Aa, kɛkɔdɔlu kɔnɔnyafɔlɔ lajikitɔ.
Aa! The first child from the first marriage was about to be circumcised.

Dimi ma to basi dɔ.
Patience will relieve every barrier.

Tan-tɛ-n kɔnɔ n'a bɛ kɛla tan wo, dinya di fɛrɛ dɔɔni.
If everybody was treated like me, life would be more peaceful.

A ko n'a bɛ kɛla jonjonjonyi la tan wo, dinya di fɛrɛ dɔɔni.
If a runaway was treated that way, life would be more peaceful.

N'a bɛ kɛla kɛdɔbanmosoyi la tan wo, dinya di fɛrɛ dɔɔni.
If a woman who abandons her husband was treated that way, life would be more peaceful.

Kanja Burema le n'a bɛ kɛla tan, dinya di fɛrɛ dɔɔni.
Kanja Burema, if it always would end like this, life would be more peaceful.

A ko n'a bɛ kɛla kɛdɔbanmosoyi la tan wo, dinya di fɛrɛ dɔɔni.
If a woman who abandons her husband was treated this way, life would be more peaceful.

Aa, n'a bɛ kɛla tan, dinya di fɛrɛ dɔɔni.
If it would always end like this, life would be more peaceful.

N'a bɛ kɛla kɛdɔbanmosoyi la tan wo, dinya di fɛrɛ dɔɔni.
If a woman who abandons her husband was treated this way, life would be more peaceful.
[the following is in speech mode]

Mali kɛlasikimosolu le bɛɛ ka fudu mara wo, i kana niminsa.
Married women of Mali, you all should take care of your marriage, or you will later regret it.

Aa, bɛɛ ka fudu mara, i kana niminsa.
Everybody should take care of their marriage, or they will later regret it.

Mosoninmɛsɛnnu le bɛɛ ka fudu mara wo, i kana niminsa.
Young women, you all should take care of your marriage, or you will later regret it.

References

Camara, B. (2002) "La femme dans les chansons de Siramori Jabaté" (conference paper, *Fifth International Conference on Mande Studies*, Leiden, 17–21 June).

Camara, B. and Jansen, J. (2013) "A Heroic Performance by Siramori Diabaté in Mali", in: Hale, T. A. and Sidikou, A. G. (eds.) *Women's Songs from West Africa* (Bloomington/Indianapolis, Indiana University Press): 136–151.

Camara, M. S. (2005) *His Master's Voice: Mass Communication and Single Party Politics in Guinea under Sékou Touré* (Trenton NJ, Africa World Press).

Charry, E. (2000) *Mande Music: Traditional and Modern Music of the Maninka and Mandinka of Western Africa* (Chicago, University of Chicago Press).

Counsel, G. (2009) "Digitising and Archiving Syliphone Recordings in Guinea", *Australasian Review of African Studies* 30–1: 144–150.

— (2010) "Music for a Coup — 'Armée Guinéenne'. An Overview of Guinea's Recent Political Turmoil", *Australasian Review of African Studies* 31–2: 94–112.

— (2012) "Conserving the Archives of a National Broadcaster", *Context* 37: 121–127.

— (2013) "The Music Archives of Guinea: Nationalism and its Representation under Sékou Touré" (conference proceedings: *African Renaissance and Australia*, Murdoch University), http://afsaap.org.au/assets/graeme_counsel.pdf

— (2015) "Music for a Revolution: The Sound Archives of Radio Télévision Guinée", in: Kaminko, M. (ed.) *From Dust to Digital: Ten Years of the Endangered Archives Programme* (Cambridge, Open Book Publishers): 547–586, http://dx.doi.org/10.11647/OBP.0052; http://www.openbookpublishers.com/reader/283/#page/616/mode/1up

Counsel, G., Jansen, J. and Camara, B. (forthcoming in the *Journal of West African History*) "Sex, Drugs, and Diplomacy — Why Siramori Diabaté's Song 'Nanyuman' Was Such a Success in Mali and Guinea".

Derive, J. (2008) "Belles choses, belles femmes, belle langue: objets et critères de l'appréciation esthétique chez les Dioula", in: Boyeldieu, P. and Nougayrol, P. (eds.) *Langues et cultures: terrains d'Afrique, Hommage à France Cloarec-Heiss* (Louvain-Paris, Peeters), 89–98.

Diabaté, Siramori. *Sòròfè* [n.d.] (Bamako, Editions Jamana [audio cassette]).

Durán, L. (2007) "Ngaraya: Women and Musical Mastery in Mali", *Bulletin of SOAS* 70–3: 569–602.

Goffman, E. (1990 [1959]) *The Representation of Self in Everyday Life* (Harmondsworth, Penguin).

Hale, T. A. and Sidikou, A. G. (eds.) (2013) *Women's Songs from West Africa* (Bloomington/Indianapolis, Indiana University Press).

Hoffman, B. H. (2001) *Griots at War — Conflict, Conciliation, and Caste in Mande* (Bloomington, Indiana University Press).

Jansen, J. (1996) "'Elle Connaît Tout le Mande' — A Tribute to the Griotte Siramori Diabaté", *Research in African Literatures* 27–4: 198–216.

— (2012) "'Copy Debts'? Towards a Cultural Model for Researchers' Accountability in an Age of Web Democracy", *Oral Tradition* 27–2: 351–362.

Sidikou, A. G. and Hale, T. A. (2012) *Women's Voices from West Africa — An Anthology of Songs from the Sahel* (Bloomington/Indianapolis, Indiana University Press).

Simonis, F. (2015) "Le griot, l'historien, le chasseur et l'UNESCO", *Ultramarines* 28: 12–31.

Siramori Diabaté — Griot Music from Mali #3 (2002 [CD with field recordings by Jan Jansen from 1988–1989 and by John Johnson from 1973–1974]) (Leiden, PAN records 2104).

Skinner, R. T. (2012) "Cultural Politics in the Post-Colony: Music, Nationalism and Statism in Mali, 1964–75", *Africa* 82–4: 511–534.

Smith, E. (2010) *Les arts de faire société. Parentés à plaisanterie et constructions identitaires en Afrique de l'ouest (Sénégal)* (Paris, IEP).

Video references

Diabaté, Siramori (ca 1985), "Nanyuman", https://youtu.be/cb7PAdTryxQ

Kouyaté, Sory Kandia et l'Ensemble Instrumental de la Radiodiffusion Nationale (1977), "No title", https://youtu.be/L3RJk1Ld-bU

— "Touyendé", https://youtu.be/-R0gxpvhosw

— "PDG", https://youtu.be/YSPEuXBGBKM

5. New Electronic Resources for Texts in Manding Languages

Valentin Vydrin

Introduction[1]

Since 2009, there has been continuous work conducted on electronic resources for Manding languages in Western Africa. In 2011, a Bamana Reference Corpus (Corpus Bambara de Référence) was published online (Vydrin, Maslinsky, Méric *et al.* 2011–2017), and as of March 2017 it accounts for 3,846,094 words, about 700,000 of these being within the disambiguated subcorpus.[2] In November 2014, a Bamana Electronic Library was made available online.[3] A Maninka Corpus was opened to the public in April 2016 (Vydrin, Maslinsky, Rovenchak *et al.*, 2016–2017), and a Maninka Electronic Library was open to the public at the end of 2016.[4]

1 This work is supported by a public grant overseen by the French National Research Agency (ANR) as part of the "Investissements d'Avenir" program (reference: ANR-10-LABX-0083).

2 All the texts in the Corpus are automatically annotated for part of speech tags and for French glosses; the automatic annotation is based on a lexical database (electronic dictionary), Bamada, and on a formalized set of morphological rules. Originally, in the automatically analyzed texts, more than 70% of all words were annotated ambiguously (i.e. more than one variant of analysis was produced by the program); recently, thanks to the improvement of our electronic tools, this rate was reduced to 60%. At the next stage, the texts are treated (disambiguated) by human operators who should have a good knowledge of Bamana language and Bamana grammar; they select the correct analyses among those suggested by the automatic analyser, or produce them (if no correct analysis is suggested by the program).

3 http://cormand.huma-num.fr/biblio/

4 http://cormand.huma-num.fr/maninkabiblio/index.jsp

 https://doi.org/10.11647/OBP.0111.05

Manding is a large language/dialect continuum in Western Sub-Saharan Africa (see Map 5.1). The entire Manding speaking population is close to forty million, placing it among the most important languages of Africa. Manding (in some publications, also stylised as Mandingo) is a generic name for a great number of language varieties, among which the biggest ones are Bamana/Bamanakan (also Bambara) in Mali, Maninka (also Malinke) in Guinea, Mali, Senegal, and Sierra-Leone, Mandinka in Gambia, Senegal and Guinea-Bissau, and Jula in Côte d'Ivoire and Burkina Faso. These varieties are usually regarded as individual languages, and separate written norms are emerging in spite of certain harmonisation efforts by linguists.

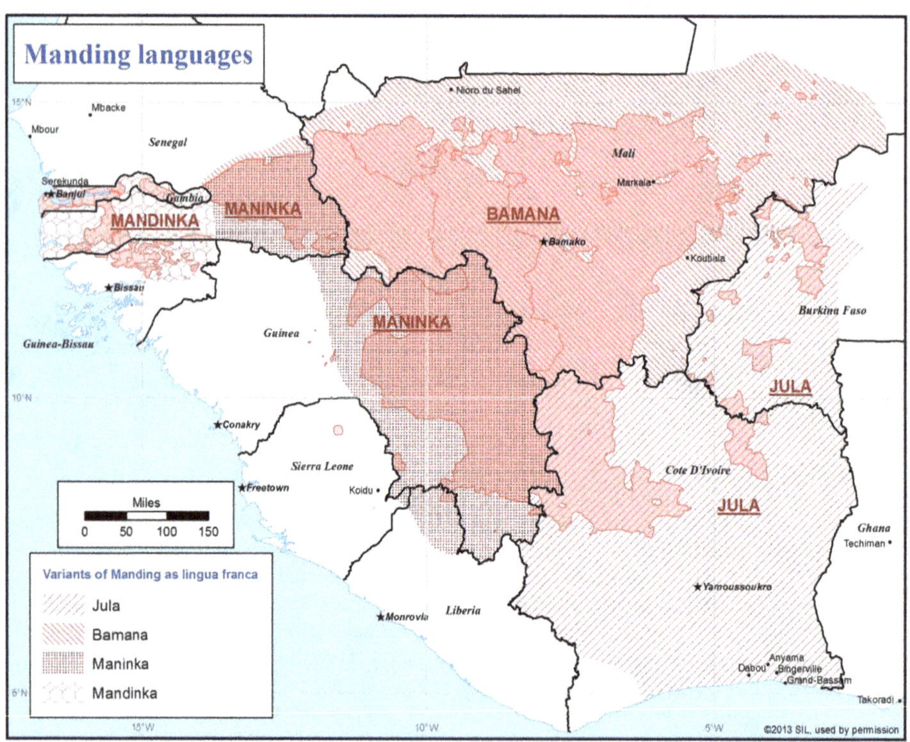

Fig. 5.1 Major Manding varieties. The light hatching covers the areas where Manding varieties are used as *lingua franca*. © 2004 SIL International, used with permission, redistribution not permitted.

In this chapter I will discuss the current situation regarding the collection and presentation of texts in the main Manding varieties in Mali (Bambara) and Guinea (Maninka). The resources in question deal mainly with written texts, and only marginally with audio texts. While this diverges from the main topic of this volume, it may still be of interest to the audience.

The Bambara Library

The availability of texts in Manding languages in Mali is ambiguous. On one hand, Bambara is the country's most prominent language, spoken by 80% of the population, and is well represented in electronic mass media. There is a written press in Bambara: the *Kibaru* monthly has existed since 1971, the *Jɛkabaara* monthly has existed since 1984, and a number of other periodicals have been launched (but disappeared more or less quickly). The number of books published in Bambara in Mali is considerable: in my bibliographic database, which is not exhaustive, there are five hundred Malian publications. While this may not be very impressive for a language with more than twelve million speakers (and even ridiculous if compared with the written output in any small language of Europe, such as Estonian or Latvian), it is still significant if we take into account the fact that Mali is firmly entrenched in the bottom twenty countries of the Human Development Index. Bambara does not have official language status in the Republic of Mali, is not used in administration, and is used only marginally in the education system. Among these books, booklets predominate; only around fifty books in my database exceed one hundred pages. Included in these are textbooks and religious books, but also a number of fiction books and collections of oral literature texts. While it is too early to discuss a fully-fledged written literature, an embryo literature does exist.[5]

Despite the hundreds of publications in Bambara, it is not an exaggeration to say that the language remains almost exclusively an oral one. Bambara publications are practically invisible in bookshops

5 For a survey of literatures in Manding languages, see the page *Littérature en mandingue* by Jean Derive on the ELLAF website, http://ellaf.huma-num.fr/langues-et-litteratures/mandingue-2 (Derive 2016). For some reasons, in the first version of the site of ELLAF, there is no mention of the literature in Nko.

(which are quite rare even in Bamako, let alone in provincial centers), in the small number of libraries, and in schools. The periodicals in Bambara are absent from the newsstands. Households where books in Bambara can be found are few and far between. For the great majority of Malians, Bambara remains an unwritten language.

In rare instances where Manding is involved in a commercial sphere,[6] namely in the transcription of song lyrics on the CDs of popular singers, Bambara is usually treated as a language without any written norm. The texts are written using a French-based "orthography". Some examples of this are: *gn* is used for *ɲ*, there is no distinction between the semi-closed and semi-open vowels *e* and *ɛ*, the vowel length is ignored, there is no standard regarding the rules of word segmentation, etc. Furthermore, when my students contacted a popular singer to offer help with the transcription of song texts, the reaction was negative and even hostile.

Evidently, the written variant of Bambara is trapped in a vicious cycle. Written documents in Bambara are (almost) unavailable, causing people not to consider Bambara as a written language. As a result, publications in Bambara have no audience, appearing rarely in tiny print runs and disappearing soon afterwards almost without a trace. Very little impact and no cumulative effect is observed.

The "Bibliothèque Électronique Bambara" project was conceived in June 2014 by scholars from Langage, Langues et Cultures d'Afrique Noire (LLACAN), a CNRS laboratory where I work, and the Académie Malienne des Langues (AMALAN) as an attempt to curb this negative tendency. The idea was very simple: to make as many Bambara documents as possible, of any genre, available in Open Access mode. In November 2014, the Bibliothèque Électronique Bambara website was launched.[7]

From the very beginning, the project was intended as not-for-profit; it had a non-existent budget. So far, I have scanned almost all of the documents posted on the site; a small number of the documents (in PDF format) have been contributed by their authors and editors. The

6 Otherwise, publications in Bambara in Mali are most often sponsored by official structures or by non-profit NGOs. Publishing houses producing Bambara books, as a rule, do it with grant money, therefore these publications do not really represent a profit-oriented sector.

7 See http://cormand.huma-num.fr/biblio/index.jsp. The site has been developed and is maintained by Tahar Meddour, a computer engineer from LLACAN.

website consists of three sections: "Ouvrages", "Publications bilingues", and "Périodiques". At the site's launch, 167 books were posted in the "Ouvrages" section, and among these 68 were downloadable with the others being in "partial display" mode (a couple of initial pages are shown in a non-downloadable format). These numbers are constantly growing.

In 2015, I obtained a "promotion grant" from the LabEx Empirical Foundations of Linguistics which allowed me to delegate the job of scanning Bambara (and also Nko) books to a student. When the extent of my personal library comes to an end, I plan to scan the personal library of Gérard Dumestre.[8] I count on the help of other colleagues, as well as the public and university libraries in European countries, where Bambara books tend to remain safer than in the harsh Sahelian environment. Our AMALAN partners assist in the task of making publications (and other documents) available in the Library, and in handling the copyright questions with (mostly) Malian authors and publishers.

Most of the downloadable books are published by the Direction Nationale de l'Alphabétisation Fonctionnelle et Linguistique Appliquée (DNAFLA), which was the name of Mali's national literacy agency until the end of 1990s, and by other governmental bodies whose work can be considered copyright-free (AMALAN is an heir of DNAFLA). For the other publications (about 60% of the collection), negotiations are ongoing with authors and publishers, and the "partial display" mode is a temporary solution that enables the books to be listed on the website. It is natural for authors and publishers to want to earn a profit through book sales, and for them to refrain from posting their material to access freely on the internet. However, the lack of dynamism within the Bambara book market makes profit-oriented publishing very difficult: Malians, with some rare exceptions, do not tend to buy books (apart from religious books, textbooks, and other publications necessary for their careers or another practical purpose). Therefore, after a relatively short period following publication, the copyright holder would be unlikely to lose any potential profit if the book is available to access for free on the internet. In any case, I try to convince the copyright holders to allow online access once a book runs out of print, in order to save it from oblivion.

8 Gérard Dumestre was the professor of Manding languages at INALCO until 2010; his personal library of publications in Bambara is probably the richest in the world.

Documents posted in the section "Publications bilingues" are academic publications which appeared mainly in Europe. For a while, this section has been very modest, but we hope to augment it with contributions from colleagues willing to make their works available for a wider audience. In the section "Périodiques", almost all of the Bambara periodicals I know of are represented: *Kibaru*, *Jɛkabaara*, *Kalamɛnɛ*, *Jama*, *Kolonkisɛ*, *Nafarinma*, *Ntuloma*, *Ɲɛtaa*, *Saheli*, *Sankore*, and *Faso Kumakan* (a weekly Bambara supplement to the official newspaper *l'Essor* during the 1980s). In November 2014, when the Bibliothèque was launched, about 180 issues were posted; this number is constantly growing. We are also planning to create a section called "First Publication", where previously unpublished Bambara texts will be posted (for example, recordings of various genres of oral tradition).

The Cross-Fertilisation of the Bibliothèque Électronique Bambara and the Corpus Bambara de Référence

Who will use the Bibliothèque Électronique Bambara? The main visitors will be students of the Bambara languages in European universities (Paris, St. Petersburg, Bayreuth, Mainz, Köln, Wien, and others) and in North America (Bloomington, Chicago, Boston, for example), as well as fully-fledged Manding specialists. The big question is: will the Bibliothèque remain an "expatriate club" unnoticed by Malians, or will it also be consulted by at least some members of the Malian intellectual elite? The latter is not impossible; I have already received emails from Malians studying in France asking for various publications in Bambara, and I have redirected them, with pleasure, to the Bibliothèque website. But will it become popular among the Malians who visit internet cafés in Bamako and Ségou? Or among village dwellers who connect to the internet by the means of a GPRS or 3G modem? I hope that the Bibliothèque will play some role in the preservation of the Manding cultural heritage, and that at least some Malians will read the books and newspapers downloaded from our site.[9]

9 We began using Google Analytics to track the number of visitors to the Bambara Electronic Library in February 2016. During one month, more than 3,500 documents

The Bibliothèque Électronique Bambara is a small part of a global project of Bambara language documentation. The Corpus Bambara de Référence is the larger component, an annotated electronic corpus of texts: http://cormand.huma-num.fr. So far, to my knowledge, it is the only open-access mid-size corpus of a language from Sub-Sahara Africa. I hope, and expect, that the Bibliothèque Électronique Bambara will profit from a cross-fertilisation with the Corpus Bambara de Référence.

The Corpus is a much more time-consuming project than the Electronic Library, and it is also a powerful analytical tool. All of the texts included in the Corpus contain detailed metatextual information, and every word and morpheme is annotated to identify the tone[10] and the part of speech characteristics, and provided with a gloss (a simplified French translation equivalent). For the major part of the Corpus (about 85%), the annotation is automatically performed by a morphological analyser based on the electronic Bamana-French dictionary "Bamadaba"[11] and a set of morphological rules. About 15% of the Corpus has been disambiguated semi-manually; the disambiguated subcorpus can be used for much more subtle searches.[12] In March 2017, the entire Bambara Corpus contained 3,846,094 words. At the same time, the disambiguated subcorpus consisted of about 700,000 words (these figures are constantly growing).

The Bambara Reference Corpus is, first and foremost, a powerful tool for linguistic studies. It allows for much more fine-grained research than in the pre-corpus era. In particular, the Corpus was used intensively to elaborate the proposals for the Bambara orthography (Konta and Vydrin 2014), while many questions which would otherwise require

were downloaded or consulted; there were 110 visits by 83 visitors. The distribution of visits was as follows: France 48, Mali 10, Russia 10, US 6, UK 5, Germany 3, Guinea 3, Sudan 3, etc. The total number of visits from African countries was 22, i.e. 20%.

10 Bambara is a tonal language, but in the published texts tones are usually not marked.

11 http://cormand.huma-num.fr/bamadaba.html

12 To illustrate the difference between the disambiguated and non-disambiguated subcorpora, it is enough to say that about 70% of all the words in a non-disambiguated Bambara text (originally without tonal marks) have two or more variants of translation. This is due to a set of factors, such as: abundant homonymy and (for toneless texts) quasi-homonymy; extremely scarce inflectional morphology and productive parts of speech conversion; and very productive word compounding.

tedious studies and long discussions found more or less quick and convincing solutions.[13] It is used heavily in Bambara language teaching in European universities, with great effectiveness. A path is open for a corpus-driven Bambara dictionary, where every word and meaning will include statistical information about its representation in the Corpus. A corpus-driven dictionary would be labour-intensive, but at the same time a very gratifying project.[14]

It would be wrong to think that the Bambara Corpus is of interest only to linguists. It can be used by specialists in all adjacent fields dealing with Bambara texts and terms: scholars from cultural, social and even political anthropology who participate in the study of written and oral literature all need to know the preferred spelling of a term from time to time. The Corpus can also be of great value since the meaning of a word may change. Various written sources are given, beginning in the 1970s (even earlier documents could be included, although such documents are rare), and special efforts are put into making the Corpus representative, as much as possible, for different periods. One can easily imagine a corpus study of the evolution of the use and meaning of key words in various fields, e.g. *fòroba* (which in the March 2016 version of the Corpus had 208 occurrences) evolved from connoting "collective farm" to "public (property)"; or *jàhadi, jìhadi* (45 occurrences) which changed from meaning "effort; holy war" (in Islam) to "catastrophe,

13 For example, the spelling of the names of deciles (the first number in each group of ten) from thirty to ninety is illustrative. These names are formed by adding the element *bî* in preposition to the respective names of the units. This element is tonally autonomous, which is mainly a characteristic of separate words, but no other word can be inserted between *bî* and the name of the unit (which is an argument in favour of the single-word interpretation). Among linguists, opinions diverge and discussions are sometimes quite fierce; in the texts, both spellings (one word or two) can be found. A corpus study in March 2016 (which took me about ten minutes) produced the following result: "30" *bi saba* — 215 occurrences, *bisaba* — 23; "40" *bi naani* — 235 occurrences, *binaani* — 32; "50" *bi duuru* — 189 occurrences, *biduuru* — 15; "60" *bi wɔɔrɔ* — 83 occurrences, *biwɔɔrɔ* — 7; "70" *bi wolonwula* — 114 occurrences, *biwolonwula* — 0; "80" *bi segin* and *bi seegin* — 66, *bisegin* and *biseegin* — 4; "90" *bi kɔnɔntɔn* and *bi kɔnɔntɔ* — 26, *bikɔnɔntɔn* — 1. The total number of split forms in the Corpus is 928, while one word spelling occurred only 82 times. Therefore, in practice, Bambara authors overwhelmingly prefer to use two words, which was also recommended by Konta and Vydrin (2014).

14 A three-million-word corpus is big enough for the study of grammar, but it is rather small for research on lexical semantics. For a medium-sized corpus-driven dictionary, at least a six- or seven-million-word corpus is usually deemed necessary.

disaster"; or yet *sáraka* (182 occurrences), which developed from "alms" to "sacrifice" or "to cast a spell".

The statistics that track visits to the Bambara Corpus show its growing popularity. In 2015, the counter recorded 861 individual visitors,[15] and 1591 visits in total. The peak of its popularity was reached in December (176 individual visitors, 404 total visits), and during the year, we observed a steady growth (with a predictable lull during the summer months). During March 2016, the number of unique visitors reached 500, and the total number of visits was close to 800. The vast majority of visitors are from Europe (mainly France, Germany and Russia), and visits from African countries are not frequent (unless they are hidden in the large category "Unknown"). Evidently, the Bambara Corpus is not only visited by specialists in the Bambara language, as the number of students of Bambara in the countries of Europe and North America is certainly far below the number of visitors to the website. We can conclude that this tool is being used more and more by specialists from adjacent disciplines and by a wide audience interested in Mali and the Bambara language in particular.

The evolution of the Corpus Bambara de Référence (besides a further growth of its size) is planned in three steps as follows:

- Building an audio-corpus of Bambara texts. Initial steps in this direction have been taken recently: Jean Jacques Méric is working on the software conversion necessary to synchronise the audio and the written texts. Building an audio-corpus is considerably more time-consuming than a written corpus, but these extra efforts allow sound, if some computer difficulties are solved, and graphs provided by speech analysis programs.
- Building a parallel subcorpus of texts (mainly Bambara-French). Currently all words and morphemes in the Bambara Corpus are annotated with part of speech tags and with French glosses), but no free translations of phrases are available. This means the use of the Corpus by those who have no command of Bambara is

15 This figure was noted down on 27 December 2015. However, there were two gaps, in April-May and September-October, when the counter did not work. The actual number of individual visitors might therefore have been well above 1,000 (the number of total visits should be increased accordingly).

difficult. In a parallel corpus, every Bambara sentence will be provided with its French equivalent. Even for those who speak Bambara perfectly, such a subcorpus will facilitate the possibility of searching for French idiomatic expressions, for example. A parallel corpus has great potential for language technologies, and in particular, for the development of automatic translation programs.

- Development of an automatic statistic-based disambiguation tool. Such a tool will reduce the rate of ambiguous annotations in the main subcorpus. The first steps for this were taken in 2015.

The Maninka Library for Guinea

We also intend to expand the existing model of electronic resources to closely related languages, starting with Guinean Maninka. The situation in Guinea regarding literature and other sources in the Manding languages is rather peculiar. During the period of the First Republic (1958–1984), an attempt was made to introduce local languages in education as much as possible, as well as in all other spheres of life. However, this initiative was not properly prepared. In my collection, there are only seven books in Maninka published during this period: school textbooks, primers for adults, and functional literacy books about stockbreeding; no fiction or oral literature is available. Most likely, other publications did exist, but disappeared without a trace. After the death of the first president Sékou Touré, education in the national languages was abandoned altogether; it was maintained only for small-scale adult literacy programs, and only two to three dozen Maninka books have appeared in Guinea since 1984 using the reformed Latin script.[16]

However, there is a written tradition in Nko writing, in which an original alphabet for Manding has existed since 1949 when it was introduced by Solomana Kantè. The alphabet began to flourish after 1984, mainly in Guinea, but also in neighbouring countries.[17] Today, the number of people literate in Nko can be counted in the hundreds of

16 Letters for semi-open vowels *è*, *ö* were replaced by *ɛ*, *ɔ* respectively; the digraphs *ty*, *dy*, *ny* by single letters *c*, *j*, *ɲ*.

17 The history and practice of Nko has been dealt with in numerous publications, for instance Amselle (2001); Oyler (2001); Vydrine (2001, 2011); Wyrod (2008).

thousands; there are several periodicals in Nko,[18] and there are more than four hundred Nko book titles in my database.

In co-operation with Guinean colleagues from the IRLA (Institut de Recherches Linguistiques Appliquées) and *Ńkó Dúnbu* (the Nko Academy), a Maninka Electronic Library project which includes books and periodicals was open for public at the end of 2016 (http://cormand.huma-num.fr/maninkabiblio/index.jsp). It follows the same model as the Bambara Library. In contrast to Bambara Latin-based writing, Nko enjoys broad popularity. The publication of books in Nko is often sponsored by individuals and the books are distributed as photocopies all over Guinea. They are often available in provincial Nko bookshops years after publication, and many people keep them in their own collections. Undoubtedly, the preservation of Nko literature is much more advanced than that of Bambara literature, although this does not mean there is no need for an electronic library.

An important question in relation to such an open-access resource is the attitude of the Nko authors. Among Nko authors and publishers, the question of copyright is significant, and cases of copyright-related conflicts concerning the intellectual heritage of Solomana Kantè have been attested. Taking into account the often mistrustful attitude of some Nko militants towards the Western world, a reserved attitude of certain authors toward the project is understandable. However, the Nko movement is far from homogeneous. Side by side with hardened Third World activists who distrust external initiatives, one can find inviting people — often from a western academic background — who have a positive experience of co-operation with outsiders. Fortunately, the attitude of *Ńkó Dúnbu* (the Nko Academy) has been extremely positive towards our projects from the very beginning, and its Academic Secretary, Ibrahima Sory II Condé, has contact authors, collected electronic versions of their books, and requested permission for the inclusion of their works in the Electronic Library. It is also important that from the very beginning, the Electronic Library has been conceived as a joint project with *Ńkó Dúnbu*, which helped to convince those who were initially reluctant and feared a wicked scheme designed to rob the Nko people of their intellectual wealth.

18 In 2012, *Dálilu Kɛ́ndɛ* became the first weekly publication in Maninka, and for a while it managed to surpass all other periodicals in Guinea (appearing in French) with its print-run of 3,000 copies.

Conclusion

When this chapter was first composed, I wrote: "A Maninka Corpus can also be developed in the future". At the time of publishing, this corpus is available online (since April 2016) and Open Access at http://cormand.huma-num.fr/cormani. It includes two subcorpora, "Corpus Nko", which includes texts originally created in Nko writing, and "Corpus Manika", originally in the Latin alphabet. The Nko subcorpus has reached 3,122,178 words, and the Latin-based Maninka subcorpus contains 396,389 words.[19] Both Nko and Maninka subcorpora are available in Nko and in Latin-based alphabets (the convertors have been developed by Andrij Rovenchak). The software package Daba described earlier, devised by Kirill Maslinsky for the Bambara Corpus, has been adapted by him for the Mandinka Corpus. Kirill Maslinsky and Andrij Rovenchak, who has done excellent work in converting Nko publications into electronic texts, have combined three sources for the development of the Maninka electronic database: an enlarged version of Vydrin's dictionary (Vydrine 1999); a word frequency list generated on the basis of the preliminary version of the Nko Corpus containing two million words; and an electronic version of the French-Nko Dictionary (Kantè 2012). The resulting electronic dictionary, Malidaba, is used for the morphological analysis of the Maninka/Nko Corpus. A "cleansing" of Malidaba is being carried out, which consists mainly of the elimination of duplicates and providing all the entries with French, English and Russian glosses. In April 2016, when the first version of the Maninka Corpus was published online, some 15% of the Malidaba had been cleansed; in March 2017, when the second update of the Corpus took place, this rate reached 54%.

Thanks to computer technology, written versions of African languages have been exposed to a rapid progress. The Bambara and Maninka projects may serve as models for other languages of the region.

---

19 A large part of the collection and conversion (first into UNICODE fonts, then from Nko to Latin transliteration) was done by Andrij Rovenchak. A great number of texts were contributed in different electronic formats by members of the Nko Academy (*Ńkó Dúnbu*) and other authors; this collection was organised by Ibrahima Sory II Condé.

References

Amselle, J. L. (2001) *Branchements. Anthropologie de l'universalité des cultures* (Paris, Flammarion).

Derive, J. (2016) "Littérature en mandingue", http://ellaf.huma-num.fr/langues-et-litteratures/mandingue-2

Kantè, S. (2012) *Dictionnaire bilingue français-n'ko/Kodofolan Faransi-N'ko* (Conakry, Académie N'ko).

Konta, M. and Vydrin, V. (2014) "Propositions pour l'orthographe du bamanankan", *Mandenkan* 52: 22–54.

Maslinsky, K. (2014) "Daba: A Model and Tools for Manding Corpora", in: Mangeot, M. and Sadat, F. (eds.) *Actes de l'atelier sur le traitement automatique des langues africaines TALAf 2014*, http://talaf.imag.fr/2014/Actes/MASLINSKY - Daba%3B a model and tools for Manding corpora.pdf

Oyler, D. (2001) "The Era of Mande Enlightenment", *Mande Studies* 3: 75–94.

Vydrin(e), V. (1999) *Manding-English Dictionary (Maninka, Bamana)*, vol. 1 (St. Petersburg, Dmitry Bulanin Publishing House).

— (2001) "Soulemane Kantè, un philosophe-innovateur traditionaliste maninka, vu à travers ses écrits en Nko", *Mande Studies* 3: 99–131.

— (2011) "L'alternative du N'ko: une langue écrite mandingue commune, est-elle possible?", in: Lexander, K. V., Lyche, C. and Moseng Knutsen, A. (eds.) *Pluralité des langues pluralité des cultures: regards sur l'Afrique et au-delà* (Oslo, The Institute for Comparative Research in Human Culture): 195–204.

— (2012) "Une bibliographie préliminaire des publications maninka en écriture N'ko", *Mandenkan* 48: 59–121.

Vydrin V., Maslinsky K., Méric J. J. *et al.* (2011–2017) Corpus Bambara de Référence, http://cormand.huma-num.fr

Vydrin, Maslinsky, Rovenchak *et al.* (2016–2017) Corpus Maninka de Référence et Corpus N'ko, http://cormand.huma-num.fr/cormani/projet.html

Wyrod, C. T. (2008) "A Social Orthography of Identity: The N'ko Literacy Movement in West Africa", *International Journal of the Sociology of Language* 192: 27–44.

6. Questioning "Restitution": Oral Literature in Madagascar

Brigitte Rasoloniaina and Andriamanivohasina Rakotomalala

Introduction[1]

This chapter argues that the restitution of oral heritage in Madagascar has a long history, and reveals itself in different ways through various research agendas over time. This is influenced by the socio-political context and the available recording technologies. The Malagasy language was written in Latin characters from an early date in the nineteenth century, so traditional oral literature (such as tales and proverbs) was mainly circulated by written works. These were originally published by missionaries, then by scholars and academics. Schoolbooks that reproduced these texts for young generations have a limited impact at present. Today, the production of documents with sound and pictures

1 We would like to thank Sarah Fee, Melissa Metcalf and Madeleine Tesseraud for their assistance, including translation from French. The bibliographical references on Malagasy Folktale (see Appendix) are mostly taken from an unpublished paper "Bibliographie du conte populaire à Madagascar", presented by Serge H. Rodin, Noël J. Gueunier and a group of students, at the International Symposium "Contes, mythes et traditions populaires de Madagascar et des Mascareignes", 5–7 September 2005, University of Antananarivo, Faculty of Letters and Human Sciences.

 https://doi.org/10.11647/OBP.0111.06

(documentary films, etc.) might be a way to recover these texts for the local population.

Researchers in anthropology and oral traditions often pose questions about the "restitution" or the "return" of data from field recordings to the communities where they were collected and where the producers or authors live. The debate about"restitution" has recently received a lot of attention (Glowczewski 2005, 2009; Bell *et al.* 2013). We aim to illustrate, on the basis of oral literature research in Madagascar, that many of the issues raised are not new; some of the questions even date back to Evans-Pritchard's research in the 1950s (Evans-Pritchard 1969: chapter 6).

Oral literature in Madagascar is a valuable case study for an examination of these topics, particularly given the history of literacy, of the collection of traditional heritage, and of book publishing in this country, which has a longer history than publishing in other formerly colonised countries in sub-Sahara Africa.

To describe the modalities of this "restitution" to the people responsible for literary production in Madagascar, as well as the ways in which restitution itself has evolved over time, we begin with the work of the first Malagasy scholars and European Christian missionaries who brought forth a system of writing. These groups were followed by colonial intellectuals and, later, the initiatives of academic researchers. The collection and transcription of oral literature was originally limited almost uniquely to the central region around the capital, Antananarivo, but then spread to all regions of Madagascar (see Appendix). Most recently, the use of film recording has considerably increased the means to archive this rich oral patrimony. This chapter explores the impact of these new documentary formats from the perspective of restitution.

Collecting Data in the Nineteenth Century and the Colonial Period

In the 1820s, Latin script was introduced to the capital city of Antananarivo, when King Radama I was expanding his power over the small region of the central highlands to create a larger kingdom in Madagascar. Radama's project was recognised and supported by Great

Britain, which was the hegemonic political power in the Indian Ocean at that point. Protestant missionaries belonging to the London Missionary Society (LMS) introduced this technical innovation,[2] seeing in it a useful means of evangelisation. It complemented the King's ambition to provide a program of modernisation and territorial conquest. The literacy campaign that rapidly ensued had definite consequences. It made the standardization of a literary Malagasy language possible, originally based on the dialect of central Madagascar, and it established a small literary group in the midst of the royal court.

The first generation of missionaries concentrated on the massive project of translating the Bible and composing the first dictionary, which were both published in 1835; they showed no particular interest in literary oral traditions (Raison 1977; Raison-Jourde 1991: 574–577). However, their educated pupils, the first Malagasy intellectuals, began the collection of this material. It was under Ranavalona I, the queen who succeeded Radama, that Malagasy scholars accumulated the first collections of proverbs (*ohabolana*), poetical content rich in metaphors (*hainteny*), tales (*angano*), and historical narratives (*tantara*) comprising the memorization of public discourse (*kabary*) by the most famous kings of the past. The paradox is that, although Ranavalona had cut ties with the Europeans and expelled missionaries, it was precisely during this period that the educated elite used their new skills as writers to publish their works. The manuscript notebooks they filled were discovered after the re-opening of the Kingdom to Europeans in the 1860s, by a new generation of missionaries who were well aware of their importance.[3] It was then that the first printed collections of oral traditions were published and became the classics of Malagasy literature. Notable

---

2 Writing was already present in Madagascar in the form of the Arab alphabet introduced several centuries earlier. But the script had only been used for very limited social purposes, the scribes being recruited from small aristocratic groups. Although the manuscripts they produced (known as "*sorabe*") occasionally included transcriptions of oral traditions, their very limited dissemination excludes them from our study.

3 Some remained unpublished and reappeared only later, sometimes as result of recent research. It was only after independence that the oldest collection of *hainteny* was published. This manuscript originated from the early days of the reign of Ranavalona, and was previously kept in a private family collection (Domenichini-Ramiaramanana 1968).

collections of tales from that era include those edited by the Norwegian Lutheran missionary L. Dahle (1877), the proverbs edited by the British missionaries W. E. Cousins and J. Parrett (1871), and the *History of the Kings*, a set of manuscripts collated and completed using oral research by the French Jesuit F. Callet (a first edition in 1873 was followed by several others). Malagasy authors also contributed to these publications. They included Rabezandrina, who printed a brochure in 1875 containing the tale of the tricksters Ikotofetsy and Imahaka, which is still one of the most popular traditional stories to date. The same author was later known as Rainandriamampandry, a pastor and minister in the Royal government. On the eve of his execution, by order of Gallieni, the first Governor General of the colony of Madagascar, he published a collection called *History and Traditional Customs* (1896).

The status of Malagasy as the language of communication and education was thus reinforced by this rich literature. In this period, only texts in Malagasy were published, and the classical collections mentioned above were not accompanied by a translation in a European language, their editors not judging it useful. Father Callet explicitly addressed his historic book to the Malagasy public, including this warning at the beginning:

> Oh Merina, often examine and read the history and the customs of your ancestors. History, if it is read slowly and with attention is beneficial, it provides trustworthy thoughts for what must be undertaken. [...] History is impartial: let it be said, acts which were acceptable and those which were not, if it is not today it will be to-morrow, whatever may be those who committed. So, read the history that relates to the reigns of your ancestors. (1973 [1908]: 3)[4]

Callet insisted that these injunctions — characteristic of an early concern for restitution — were taken from a manuscript written by "an old Malagasy" i.e. a student of the first schools. On the other hand, the Protestant missionaries, who had published proverbs (Cousins and Parret) and tales (Dahle) declared that they targeted an exclusively European public: they wanted to provide texts for study by their missionary colleagues who had to preach and write in Malagasy.

4 Our translation.

Regardless, their books turned out to be bestsellers for Malagasy scholars and later editions were distributed widely among the public.

Scholars of the Colonial Period (1885–1960)

The intellectual attitude of French colonial researchers was very different. This generation published remarkable collections based on oral tradition, but their general tendency was to publish only translations, usually in French. The original texts in Malagasy were either never written down or have been lost. Material was generally collected directly in French from bilingual informants. This is the case with the collection of tales by Gabriel Ferrand, a French consular government official, orientalist, and folklore specialist, which were published in 1893 when Madagascar was still a French protectorate. The translations by Ferrand are remarkable from a literary point of view; they were in some instances based on Malagasy originals previously published by missionaries, and, in some instances, on Malagasy texts which have since been lost.

Charles Renel, Director of Education in Madagascar in the early twentieth century, held an important position in the management of the colony. Through his position he was able to motivate teachers to collect a great corpus of tales. They collected manuscripts in the Malagasy language, but the publication provides only French translations *Contes de Madagascar* (1910–1930). A similar case held true for Daudouau who served as a director of a teachers' training college. His 1922 collection *Contes populaires des Sakalava et des Tsimihety de la région d'Analalava (côte Nord-Ouest de Madagascar)*, which likewise contains only translations, was collected by his students (he called them "youngsters with open spirit" in his preface, and, contrary to the habitual practice of colonial scholars, he cites the names of the most important among them). Similarly Raymond Decary, a colonial administrator for the first half of the twentieth century, published an important volume of tales collected in French from school children *Contes et légendes du Sud-Ouest de Madagascar* (1964).

A remarkable exception in this period is Birkeli. His collection of tales *Bulletin de l'Académie Malgache* (1921–1923), and other traditional texts contain the Malagasy original versions. A Norwegian Lutheran missionary, Birkeli continued the tradition of his predecessors of the preceding century. Here, however, the tales were accompanied by a French translation. My last case, Jean Paulhan, is very particular. Although a scholar of the colonial period, his profile is very different: as a young teacher he took advantage of his appointment at the Lycée of Antananarivo to explore the Malagasy literary genre of the *hainteny*, which he made known to the educated French public *Hain-Teny merinas* (1913, 1939). The first edition of his collection is bilingual. In our view, he represents a transition into the group of academic researchers whom we discuss next. In fact, before undertaking the career of writer and editor that made him famous, Paulhan had planned to write a thesis on this Malagasy oral genre, a project he never completed.

All of these authors, in one way or another, addressed a European public with the object of making Madagascar known, from an ethnographic perspective for some, linguistic or literary for others. We shall see, however, that these efforts did not exclude a certain form of restitution aimed at a local public.

Malagasy Oral Literature in Contemporary Research

Academic researchers from many disciplines — linguists, literary writers, folklorists, and anthropologists — continued the work of collecting oral literature after the colonial scholars. They were interested in the various regions of Madagascar and deliberately set out to cover the whole of the country.

Otto C. Dahl can be credited with linking this generation to the great missionary tradition, as he arrived in Madagascar to serve in the Lutheran mission in 1929. He was also a university professor who prepared a thesis in linguistics. Quite late in his career (1968) he published a collection, *Contes malgaches en dialecte sakalava*, which although small, was remarkable for its very careful accuracy. The texts are published with a French translation. With Jaques Faublée we see the arrival of the professionally trained academic. His *Récits Bara* (1947) made known the traditions of a region rarely frequented by researchers until then. The publication is comprised of the original text and a French translation. However, in the hopes of capturing the language exactly, Faublée transcribed the texts using his own phonetic rendering rather than the historical Malagasy orthography fixed in the nineteenth century. This choice greatly hindered the distribution of the contents to the local population. Some of these tales were used later in school manuals, but first had to be retranscribed in standard orthography.

From that time forward, there was a large number of university researchers who collected oral literature. Since we are not able to discuss all of them in this chapter, we shall limit ourselves to a few representative scholars whose work exemplifies a wide variety of the formats of published oral literature. Beaujard's *Mythe et société à Madagascar (Tañala de l'Ikongo). Le Chasseur d'oiseau et la Princesse du ciel* (1991), gives a concentrated corpus of the mythology of a small region, the country of the Tañala of Ikongo. On the other hand, Gueunier's *Contes de la côte ouest de Madagascar* (1991) presents a sample of the tales collected all along the West coast of the Great Island, in several Malagasy dialects, even including the near-extinct languages of small Bantu-speaking minorities (who use dialects of Swahili and Makhuwa).

Varying approaches can be found in the works of Fulgence Fanony and François Noiret. The four volumes of Fanony (2001, 2011a, 2011b) offer a vast survey of several literary genres of the Betsimisaraka country: tales, proverbs, courting conversations and some *hainteny*, poetic pieces that he calls "circumlocutions", a rather different definition from that of the genre of the same name that we mentioned above in the Merina tradition. Noiret, alternatively, presents a comparison between a heroic account that was featured in one of the most ancient collections we have mentioned (the *Specimens of Malagasy Folklore* edited by Dahle 1877) and numerous versions of the same tale collected in several regions of the island (and even in the Comoros) in *Le Mythe d'Ibonia*.

Unlike those of the colonial period, all of these studies carried out in academic settings adopt the principle of an edition of the text in the original language, accompanied by a translation in a European language, generally French. Others have gone back to the tradition of collecting in Malagasy only, without translation. This is the case, for example, in the great undertaking of the *Awakening of Tales* (1994) by Moks Razafindramiandra that brings together 210 tales collected throughout numerous regions of the country. The aim is certainly to ensure a return to the original storytellers (whose names, moreover, are carefully listed). Unfortunately the conditions of the publication and the distribution of the volume have severely limited the spread of the work.[5]

School, a Privileged Place for Restitution

Madagascar presents a very particular case among the French colonies due to the fact that a public schooling system has existed since the 1820s, seventy years before French colonization. The tradition of an erudite elite that was literate in the local language persisted and was even further developed during the colonial period. In this context we can say that the recovery of Malagasy tales and legends in school textbooks, which were published especially for students in the colony, contributed to the return of this literature to the younger generation. It was perhaps even the most successful form of restitution. But school and children's literature has, in general, been neglected by the scholars of oral tradition. It is true that the inventory of this literature is rather difficult: it consists largely of pedagogical reviews and manuals that have not always been well-conserved by libraries.

Yet it is clear that it is the schoolbook that has ensured the return of learned collections to the people: almost all Malagasy people know *the tales*, often by oral transmission, but also often because they have read them, not in the great collections of the authors whom we mentioned previously but in school books.

The first known Malagasy reading book, *Angano* (*Tales*), published before 1834 and often reprinted, contained the translation of old European fables (such as Æsop) but also five Malagasy folk tales. This collection of short stories was rapidly distributed in school books and via oral recitations, which ensured the "restitution to the people". In the 1890s, Ferrand had already discovered the oral recitations of some these tales in his survey of the storytellers on the eastern coast of the country. He was astonished that these European fables were known to illiterate people. As Gueunier has shown, fables had passed from the schoolbook into oral tradition (Gueunier 2000: 147). There is no doubt that the

5 The publication of this book was financed by the German Embassy in Madagascar. Copies were freely distributed in an administrative network but it was impossible to buy it through the normal channels.

local Malagasy tales in this collection *Angano* (pre-1834) had the same success. We find proof of this in the scholarly books of the following era. In the textbook *L'Enseignement du Français par le texte de lecture. 1ère année*, which was in use in the 1930s, we find the famous tale of *Rabotity*, "the Little Tiny Boy", a version of the international chain-tale[6] *Who is the Best?*. This time the text is given in the French translation. But it is easy to distinguish Renel's version, published in the collection destined for a learned public, from other renditions, due to the differences in the story's ending. In Renel's tale, at the end of the chain, it is not God who is the strongest of all (as expected) but instead it is Man (Penot 1934: 143). The schoolbooks have taken up this reading from generation to generation, to the point that the name of Rabotity is a reference known more or less by everyone in Madagascar.

The same mode of circulation can be seen with the reading book by Rajaobelina, *Tsingory* (1956, many reprints), which many adults today still recall nostalgically. It comprises many texts originating from oral tradition. The story which gives its title to the book was taken from the collection of tales in the Sakalava dialect from Birkeli (already quoted 1921–1923), but it is entirely rewritten in contemporary literary (standard) Malagasy. In this story of a dancer, who is a perpetrator of a crime but forgiven by the king due to the perfection of his art, a subtle adaptation in the rewriting introduces a musical instrument (the drum) that does not feature in the original text. The illustration of the book extends the reinterpretation: it represents a group of folkloric singer-dancers with drums and flutes, *hira gasy* (which we will discuss in the next section). It is not surprising that, today, questioned about the origin of their art, the *hira gasy* artists refer to a "form of tale perpetuated through oral tradition — on the mythical origin of the evolved form of Hira Gasy [...] the story of Tsingory the Dancer's first appearance at the Court" (Mauro 2001: 32). Thanks to the schoolbook, the old Sakalava story from the Birkeli collection became an original myth with a modern style, as well as a reference for contemporary artist groups (as it was probably a legend originated by a clan whose ritual specialty was dance). It is impossible to cite all of the school textbooks that have played a comparable role. We will only mention the *Joies et*

6 Chain-tales or cumulative tales are types of folk narrative that require repetition.

travaux de l'Ile heureuse from Inspector Carle (1952), a bilingual book in two volumes, where the same lessons are translated from one language to the other, with the same typographic disposition and illustrations. Once again popular tales are involved, including a version of the tale of the two tricksters Ikotofetsy and Imahaka. The restitution ensured by the reading of this story within schools has certainly helped to maintain the story in popular memory.

Unfortunately, current school manuals — preoccupied with applying pedagogic theories such as a "Competency-Based Approach", or "Educational Objective Approach", seem to have abandoned the idea of using the richness of traditional literature to introduce children to the world of reading. This abandonment is only partially counteracted by the initiatives of authors or associations that publish books for children. These selections are diverse, since the texts included vary from the translation of foreign tales, the creation of new tales, territory-specific compilations, and the translation of older collections.[7] But no matter the value of this new literature for Malagasy children, it will reach a more limited audience than the older schoolbooks did, because of costs and distribution problems.

Restitution through Anthropological Movies

For a long time it was thought to be necessary that broadcasting and restitution occurred through written publication, which only reached a restricted audience (researchers and teachers). But the book is not the only media able to insure the preservation and transmission of traditional oral texts — see, for example, the earliest stage of Malagasy literature discussed earlier. Film recordings allow tales to be updated, as well as the inclusion of elements involved in ritual: invocations, prayers, song lyrics, and texts of the ritualised speeches like the *kabary*. All of these, without a doubt, belong to contemporary oral literature. Film can ensure reproduction while still being mindful of the writing, since the transcription can be done in the moment or later on.

7 These include the remarkable collection of "Dodo bonimenteur", that Editions Dodo Vole published, a series of books of tales which included this entire range of textual varieties, with pieces like *Takalo* gathered from the mouth of a raconteur (Vaviroa 2014), *Cents sous de Sagesse* transcribed by a teacher and ethnographer (Babity 2014), and *Le Crocodile Rouge*, which was originally published in Birkeli's collection (2015).

We can use *hira gasy*, a "kind of show from the Central Highlands of Madagascar, combining dancing, singing, speeches and music" (Rakotomalala *et al.* 2001: 495) as an example.[8] Three noteworthy productions (Paes 1989; Mauro 1996; Rakotomalala 2014) show the style of this kind of theater — rural theater, according to Mauro. In these movies, we see artists in costume, on an open stage, putting themselves on the same level as the spectators and talking to them directly, not afraid to be spoken to themselves. Randrianary explains:

> The show is divided in several *hira* parts or songs with musical interludes. [...] However, the main point is to emphasise the importance of the art of speech. Applauding and screaming match the verbal formulas — sung, obviously, and received as preemptory words of truth. By moving in circles, each singer has the privilege to hear the personal appreciations from the spectators and reciprocally. (2001: 67)[9]

The *hira gasy*, while originating in the royal era of the nineteenth century, continues to develop today throughout all of the territories of the Antananarivo province, each of which has its own troupe or troupes (Randrianary 2001: 64). The lyrics of the songs illustrate different themes, and troupe chiefs, often poorly educated peasants, frequently include daily news and current events in their scenographies.

In his movie *Ranavalona's Worship in Anosimanjaka* (*Le culte de Ranavalona à Anosimanjaka*), Andriamanivohasina Rakotomalala (2014)[10] shows a troupe performing on the closing day of a ritual that happens once a year at Anosimanjaka. This village in a Merina province houses the tomb of the Princess Ranavalontsimitoviaminandriandehibe ("Lady-of-calm-with-no-equal-among-the-great-nobles"). Descendants and followers of the ancestral cult gather for the new year of the Malagasy calendar, in order to obtain the blessings of the deceased Princess. As we can see in the following lines, the artists remind us in their song of the need for the respect of parents: the artist sees the performance as a continuation and realization of an ancestral tradition, while the producer/cinematographer is concerned about issues of restitution.

---

8 The expression means literally "song, or game (*hira*) Malagasy (*gasy*)".

9 Our translation.

10 See the next page for an excerpt from this movie. Further extracts can be viewed here: https://youtu.be/nZby5J-NxZQ and here: https://youtu.be/xeXaUs0CqkA

Hira gasy shows the musical troupe ZanatSahondra performing on an open stage. Extract taken from the first movie of the trilogy *Le culte de Ranavalona à Anosimanjaka*, 290 minutes, 2014, shot between 1996 and 2009 in Anosimanjaka, Madagascar. Producer: Andriamanivohasina Rakotomalala. Duration: 7.40 minutes.[11]

(Third day, closure of the ritual)

(Singers in chorus:)
Miala tsiny e ry dada sy neny,
We present our apologies, Dad and Mum,
Mangata-tsodrano e fa zaza no miteny,
We ask for your blessing, for we are young and we dare to speak,
Dada sy neny,
Dad and Mum,
Afaka ny tsiny fanalan'ny vava,
Wrongs having been removed,
Mazava ny hizorana sy lala-kombana.
The road we will follow is clearly traced.
Isika olombelona dia zava-boary,
We the living, we are creatures
Teo am-piandohana dia nataony sarisary,
At the beginning we were formed,
Fotaka isika no novolavolaina,
From clay we were fashioned,

11 This video is also available on YouTube at https://youtu.be/Cu5p1iPu-yQ

Nomeny hery ary koa fofon'aina,
We were given the force and the breath of life,
Nanjary vatana ka nisy fanahy,
Having become a body and given a soul,
Nisy vehivavy ary nisy lehilahy,
There were men and there were women,
Koa izay indrindra tsy hadinoiko ilay Nahary,
For this I can not ignore the Creator,
Andriamanitra mpanjakan'ny zava-boary,
God, King of creation,
Ka hidera sy hankalaza ny anarany.
So let us praise and glorify his name.

(Refrain)
Dia mangata-tsodrano izahay ry dada,
So we ask for your blessing, Dad,
Dia mangata-tsodrano izahay ry neny.
So we ask for your blessing, Mum.

Ny votoatin'ny tantaranay anio dia ny manaja ray sy reny,
The theme of our words today is the respect of parents,
Satria izay nateraka hiaina dia tsy maintsy manam-piandohana,
For every living being has of necessity an origin,
I Abrama razan'ny Vazaha fa tsy an'ny Gasy velively,
Abraham is an ancester of the Whites but not of the Malagasy,
Isika tena gasy pirsàn Vazimba izao no niandohana,
We are Malagasy of pure stock stemming from Vazimba,
Ireo Malagasy teraka taloha dia nivavaka sy pôlitika,
The Malagasy of yore were religious but political too,
Ilay fiangonana ivavahany FJKM sy katôlika,
They frequented the Reformed Church or the Catholic,
Saiky tsy nataony ambanin-javatra ny razanay andriananahary,
But they did not neglect our venerable ancestors,
Isaky ny misy ataony dia tsaroany Andriamanitra sy razanay,
On every occasion they think of God and the ancestors,
Fa raha misy tsy salama dia tsabony amin'ny rano sy ny ravinkazo,
The ill, they care for with water and plants,
Dia mangataka mba mora hiala koa ny aretina sy tony tazo,
Then grace is asked so that fever and illness cease,
Miaraka amin'izany dia misotro ary dia matanjaka salama,
As soon as the potion is drunk strength and health are recovered,

Ary ity mba tazanina ireo mpivavaka masirasira,
Let us see those lukewarm believers,
Lazainy fa tsy misy hasina ireo razana sy ny vazimba,
Who say that neither ancestors nor Vazimba are sacred,
Lazainy fa manompo sampy ianao raha mba manasina ny anao,
They say you are "idol worshippers" when you honour your own,
F'angaha hono tsy mba razana ndry Maria mbamin-dry Josefa?
But Mary and Joseph are they not also ancestors?

(The Public)
Marin'izany!
That's true!

F'angaha hono mbola velona any ndry Jakoba sy ry Abrama?
Because they are still alive Jacob and Abraham?
Nahoana ireny no lazaina masina fa ny an'ny tena ananan-doza?
Why do they say that those ones are saints while blaming us for our own ones?
Tandremo tsy hanary ny fomban-drazan ô f'aleo mizara e ry Malagasy!
Malagasy! Beware! Let us not lose our ancestral traditions! Let us share them, they express the best of our values
Dia azy ny hasina tsara indrindra eee!
Let us give them the best consecration!
Eo !
So be it! There!

Why is there such an interest in filmed records? Apart from the undeniable attraction of the viewing itself, there are other assets. It is a restitution that takes into account the context of the piece: recording on film is the best way to restitute the performances of the informants. It is documenting an "act" that is part of the oral ritual ("speech act", cf. Austin 1962). Voices and gestures (head, eye, hand and foot movements) are also a part of that "speaking", as well as clothing styles, geographical and sociological contexts, etc. which all intertwine to create meaning. In short, for the complete restitution of oral literature, these contextual elements are essential.

In addition, the movie causes us to consider ourselves and our practices. Without getting into details on self-directed informants and on the behavior called "profilmic" (Souriau 1953: 8), the receiving local audience sees itself as a character, or as close to the characters. We can question the meaning that they give to the images when they watch the movie: do they see them as a reflection, similar to how they look at themselves in a mirror, or, on the contrary, do they think that they are watching a show?

Finally, the movie allows multiple viewings. This practical aspect isn't negligible in the context of archiving and broadcasting. However, the broadcasting of an anthropological movie isn't easy. The example of the Marie-Clémence and Cesar Paes movie, *Angano, angano… Nouvelles de Madagascar* (1989) is interesting in this respect. This movie features raconteurs from various regions in Madagascar as they tell their tales, as well as enactments of them. It was written and produced with the help of ethnologists, researchers, historians and literary scholars, but the basis of the scenario, which establishes the relationship between traditional narratives and filmed parts of daily life, is the directors' innovative, intimate and profound comprehension of the local setting. The original lyrics — in different Malagasy dialects — are translated using subtitles in French, English, Arabic, Mandarin Chinese, Spanish, Italian, and another version in literary (standard) Malagasy. It was screened in France during the Malagasy movie retrospective to an audience mainly composed of researchers; in California in 2008 to different schools (the institutional rights having been purchased by an association); and in Canada and Morocco by the directors, for the purpose of Master's-level classes. It is sold online in different languages.

In Madagascar, this movie is available at the French Institute, which purchased its rights and offers screenings in urban settings depending on the program. It has been presented at the Malagasy movie retrospective at the Antananarivo University, as well as in some venues around Middle West Madagascar, along with another movie from the same director about a group of Malagasy artists. A touring movie association has also screened it in three villages. Overall, however, this movie has not been shown in most of Madagascar, although it is fairly known outside the country.

The difficulties in reaching a large audience with the archives, in addition to this limited distribution, mean that screening the film is rarely possible. The administrative process (government-sponsored showings, for example) is often complicated and the equipment needed is non-existent in a rural setting. Internet access, when it is available, is not free in Madagascar, so watching the film on websites, webdocs or YouTube is almost impossible for those without means. As we know, circulation is the requirement for reception (cf. Bell *et al.* 2013).

Conclusion

We ask ourselves, if restitution isn't merely an issue for the academic scholar, who should archive the material in order to share and transmit it? It may be useful here to return to the reflections of Glowczewski (2005: 14), who asks: what exactly constitutes the "restitution" that we are looking for? People don't ask that their dances, songs, etc. be returned to them. It is more that the knowledge attached to those productions might be seen as "stolen" by the researchers (foreign, most of the time), given that their performances are now recorded in a medium that the artists don't understand. What is taken is not the content (lyrics, music and choreography), but rather the right to talk with authority about a practice that is not the researchers' own.

These ideas are strikingly similar to those of the traditionalist Randriamahatsiaro in the Paes movie *Angano, angano*, cited above:

> May what I say be transmitted, so it can be heard in the future history, by all the descendants, by all the sons, by all the grandsons. Take this with you; there may be a resemblance with other countries. Tales are the ears of inheritance. There might be ideas to take from all of this. I will probably end it like that. I'm thanking you to take my voice for others to remember. May [...] each nation preserve its oral tradition, so it can be heard by all the other nations.[12]

The traditionalist modestly but firmly defends an ambition: what he produced mustn't only be used to reveal to spectators the Malagasy heritage, it must also be part of an exchange where the "indigenous" (in the words of the old folklorists) aren't subsumed into an interpretative work, but become actors in this work. This way, the restitution would encourage live research, i.e. an active and permanent involvement of social actors, thus including the transmitters of the traditional project in a collaboration, and avoiding a partial process that would only satisfy scholars.

12 Our translation: "Ary hañitatry ny zavatra izay voalazako iñy, mba ho heno tantara, ho henon'ny taranaka faramandimby, ary ho entinareo koa any... kasy, raha misy itovizany amin'ny firenen-kafa izany, raha misy itovizany, aminareo izay man... anay izany tantara sy lovan-tsofina izany, ary asa koa misy hevitra tianareo tsoahina amin'izany zavatra izany. Izay angamba no amaranako an'azy, ka dia misaotra anareo izay naka feo anay niany fa mba ho tadidy sy rakitra amin'izany antony rehetra voalazako izany, ka dia [...] hitadidy tsara [anie] izay rehetra mipetaka ary samy hametraka ny lovantsofina amin'ny fireneny isany avy mba ho henon'ny firenena rehetra rehetra fa tsy ho anay ihany".

References

Austin, J. (1962) *How to Do Things with Words* (Oxford, Clarendon Press).

Bell, J., Christen, K. and Turin, M. (eds.) (2013) "After the Return: Digital Repatriation and the Circulation of Indigenous Knowledge", *Museum Anthropology Review* 7–1/2, http://josotl.indiana.edu/index.php/mar/article/view/3184/19324

Evans-Pritchard, E. E. (1969) *Anthropologie Sociale* (Paris, Payot).

Gueunier, N. J. (2000) "L'enfant qui s'enquiert de la mort, un conte malgache entre écrit et oral", in: Allibert, C. and Rajaonarimanana, N. (eds.) *L'Extraordinaire et le quotidien. Variations anthropologiques. Hommage au Professeur Pierre Vérin* (Paris, Karthala): 145–171.

Glowczewski, B. (2005) "Lines and Criss-Crossings: Hyperlinks in Australian Indigenous Narratives", *MIA (Media International Australia) Digital Anthropology* 116: 24–35 (+ DVD).

— (2009) "Restitution de données anthropologiques en multimedia: défis pratiques, éthiques et scientifiques", in: Albaladejo, C., Geslin, P., Magda, D., Salembier, P. (eds.) *La Mise à l'épreuve. Le transfert des connaissances en questions* (Paris, Editions Quæ): 69–86.

Mauro, D. (2001) *Madagascar. L'Opéra du peuple. Anthropologie d'un fait social total: l'art Hira gasy entre tradition et rébellion* (Paris, Karthala).

Raison, F. (1977) "L'Echange inégal de la langue. La pénétration des techniques linguistiques dans une civilisation de l'oral (Imerina, début du XIXe siècle)", *Annales. Economies, Sociétés, Civilisations* 32–4: 639–669.

Raison-Jourde, F. (1991) *Bible et pouvoir à Madagascar au XIXe siècle. Invention d'une identité chrétienne et construction de l'Etat (1780–1880)* (Paris, Karthala).

Rakotomalala, M., Blanchy, S., Raison-Jourde, F. (eds.) (2001) *Usages sociaux du religieux sur les Hautes Terres malgaches. Les ancêtres au quotidien* (Paris, L'Harmattan).

Randrianary, V. (2001) *Madagascar. Les chants d'une île* (Paris/Arles, Cité de la Musique/Actes Sud) [includes CD-rom].

Searle, J. (1969) *Speech Acts: An Essay in the Philosophy of Language* (Cambridge, Cambridge University Press).

Souriau, E. (ed.) (1953) *L'Univers filmique* (Paris, Flammarion).

Video references

Mauro, D. (1996) *Madagascar, la parole-poème. Chronique de l'opéra paysan* (Movimento Production, 56 minutes), https://youtu.be/Vqp5jx1KE4E

Paes, M. C. and Paes, C. (1989) *Angano, angano… Nouvelles de Madagascar* (DigiBeta/Latérit Productions, 63 minutes) https://youtu.be/LB8UNb6vjlI and https://youtu.be/xfn31MWUotA

Rakotomalala, A. (2014) *Le culte de Ranavalona à Anosimanjaka* (trilogie, Production Andriamanivohasina Rakotomalala, 290 minutes): Film 1: *Alahamady. Rituel du nouvel an, rituel politique, rituel religieux.* Film 2: *Mythes et identités. La princesse Ranavalona et le village.* Film 3: *Valeur et tradition. Culte de Ranavalona et devenir de la noblesse locale.*

Extracts from the trilogy are available on YouTube at:

https://youtu.be/Cu5p1iPu-yQ

https://youtu.be/nZby5J-NxZQ

https://youtu.be/xeXaUs0CqkA

Appendix: Selected Bibliography of Malagasy Oral Literature

This selected bibliography represents the main stages of the collection, publication, and circulation/distribution of Malagasy oral literature as it was presented in the chapter.

1. Forerunners, Missionaries and First Malagasy Scholars, Pupils of the Missionaries

Callet, F. (1873–1902) *Tantara ny Andriana eto Madagascar. Documents historiques d'après les manuscrits malgaches* (Antananarivo, Presy Katolika) (4 vols.).

Cousins, W. E. and Parrett, J. (1871) *Malagasy Proverbs* (Antananarivo, LMS). (A critical edition and French translation of this text was published by B. Domenichini-Ramiaramananana in 1971).

Dahle, L. (1877) *Specimens of Malagasy Folklore* (Antananarivo, A. Kingdon). Domenichini-Ramiaramanana, B. (1968)*Hainteny d'autrefois, poèmes traditionnels malgaches recueillis au début du règne de Ranavalona Ière 1828–1861. Haintenin'ny fahiny…* (Tananarive, Librairie Mixte).

Rabezandrina (1876) *Ikotofetsy sy Imahaka, sy Tantara Malagasy hafa koa* (Antananarivo, John Parret).

2. Colonial Period

Birkeli, E. (1921–1923) "Folklore sakalava recueilli dans la région de Morondava", *Bulletin de l'Académie Malgache*, nouvelle série VI: 185–423.

Dandouau, A. (1922) *Contes populaires des Sakalava et des Tsimihety de la région d'Analalava (côte Nord-Ouest de Madagascar)* (Alger, Jules Carbonel).

Decary, R. (1964) *Contes et légendes du Sud-Ouest de Madagascar* (Paris, Maisonneuve et Larose).

Ferrand, G. (1893) *Contes populaires malgaches* (Paris, E. Leroux).

Paulhan J. (1913) *Hain-Teny merinas* (Paris, Geuthner).

Renel, C. (1910–1930) *Contes de Madagascar* (Paris, E. Leroux) (3 vols.).

3. Academic Researchers. Recent Trends

Beaujard, P. (1991) *Mythe et société à Madagascar (Tañala de l'Ikongo). Le Chasseur d'oiseau et la Princesse du ciel* (Paris, L'Harmattan).

Dahl, O. C. (1968) *Contes malgaches en dialecte sakalava (textes, traductions, grammaire et lexique)* (Oslo, Universitetsforlaget).

Fanony, F. (2001) *Littérature orale malgache. I. L'Oiseau Grand-Tison... II. Le Tambour de l'Ogre...* (Paris, L'Harmattan) (2 vols.).

— (2011) *Öhabölaña Betsimisaraka. Proverbes Betsimisaraka* (Antananarivo, Trano Printy Fiangonana Loterana Malagasy).

— (2011) *Fankahitry (Propos galants) et Hainteny (Circonlocutions) Betsimisaraka* (Antananarivo, Trano Printy Fiangonana Loterana Malagasy).

Faublée, J. (1947) *Récits bara* (Paris, Institut d'Ethnologie).

Gueunier, N. J. (1991) *Contes de la côte ouest de Madagascar* (Paris/Antananarivo, Karthala/Ambozontany).

Noiret, F. (2008) *Le Mythe d'Ibonia, le Grand Prince (Madagascar)* (Paris, Karthala).

Razafindramiandra, M. N. (1994) *Angano malagasy nofohazina. Nangonina niaraka tamin'ny Fikambanana mikarakara ny Angano Malagasy (FIMIAMA),* (Antananarivo, Embassy of Germany).

4. School Textbooks. Children's Literature

Angano (pre-1834) (Tananarive). One booklet in twelve. Only known from the catalogue of a private library. The booklet was often reprinted in the nineteenth and twentieth centuries under the title *Angano voadikan'ny Mpianatry ny Misionary taloha* (*Tales Translated by the Pupils of the Earlier Missionaries*).

Babity, L. (2014) *Cent sous de sagesse. Mivanga fanahy* (S.l., Editions Dodo Vole).

Birkeli, E. (2015) *Voaimena, le Crocodile rouge* (S.l., Editions Dodo Vole).

Carle, R. (1952) *Joies et travaux de l'île heureuse (Cours élémentaire)/Eto Madagasikara, Nosy malalantsika* (Paris, Classiques Hachette) (2 vols.).

Pénot, S. (1934) *L'Enseignement du Français par le texte de lecture. 1ère année* (Tananarive, J. P. F. Imprimeurs-éditeurs).

Rajaobelina, P. (1956) *Tsingory, Boky famakian-teny. Cours préparatoire 1ère année* (Tananarive, Salohy).

Vaviroa, M. (2014) *Takalo* (S.l., Éditions Dodo Vole).

Afterword: Sharing Located

Mark Turin

It is a pleasure and responsibility to be the one charged with concluding this unique volume with some structured reflections on how it came into being. In so doing, I shall refrain from discussing specific contributions and individual chapters, as my co-editor, Daniela Merolla, has already handled this so effectively in her comprehensive introduction to the volume. Rather, this Afterword is offered as a closing statement that reflects on the origins, alliances and impact of the collaborative research contained in these pages.

The research collective that formed the project, entitled "Multimedia Research and Documentation of African Oral Genres: Connecting Diasporas and Local Audiences", last came together in person in December 2013, generously hosted by the Faculty of Humanities and Social Sciences (FLSH) at University Mohammed V at Agdal in Rabat and the Rabat National Library, Morocco. We are grateful to all of the participants and presenters, in particular Abdellah Bounfour (INALCO, Paris) and Khadija Mouhsine (University Mohammed V, Rabat). Beyond the contributors to this volume, we would like to thank the participants in the wider project: Abdalla Uba Adamu, Arinpe Adejumo, George Alao, Saoudé Ali, Felix Ameka, Amar Améziane, Giorgio Banti, Abdellah Bounfour, Anne-Marie Dauphin-Tinturier, Jean Derive, Geti Gelaye, Mohamed Aghali, Graham Furniss, Annekie Joubert, Roland Kießling, Khadija Mouhsine, Maarten Mous, Kamal Naït-Zerrad, Annel Pieterse, Nirhylanto Ramamonjisoa, Mechtild Reh, Mineke Schipper and Simone Tarsitani.

 https://doi.org/10.11647/OBP.0111.07

Directed by Merolla, the wider project that framed our last meeting focussed on how multimedia technologies afforded scholars new ways of sharing documentation and scientific knowledge with the cultural owners of these collected oral genres. Funded by the Netherlands Organisation for Scientific Research (NWO), the project had two distinct and overarching goals: first, to explore the use of electronic tools to reach and to "activate" larger audiences, in particular African diasporas and local publics; and second, through an iterative discussion, to offer some theoretical reflections on the nature of partnerships (between scholars, storytellers, technicians, passionate amateurs and activist documentarians) in documentation and research. As readers will already have ascertained, this edited volume speaks directly to these interrelated intellectual motivations.

Searching for Sharing is situated in a rich intellectual tradition that has long explored issues of orality, textuality, performance and cultural heritage. The digital turn, and the changing cultural landscape now so saturated with multimedia, has effectively moved the scholarly conversation from the "Preliminary Isolation of the Performative"(Austin 1962: 4) to one in which oral traditions and the internet are increasingly understood to be "homologous technologies of communication" (John Miles Foley, personal communication). As Scott has convincingly argued, the digital turn can work to facilitate the "formation of relationships of trust and cooperation, rather than those of exclusion or superiority" (2012: 2). Yet, for all of the access that digital tools afford, the conversation around sharing cultural heritage, whether in person or online, always comes back to fundamental questions of ownership, trust, ethics and collaboration.

A number of projects and interdisciplinary research initiatives are engaging with these questions in exciting and holistic ways. The Intellectual Property Issues in Cultural Heritage (IPinCH) project — a seven-year international research initiative based at Simon Fraser University in Canada — explores the rights, values, and responsibilities of material culture, cultural knowledge and the practice of heritage research.[1] Similarly, while the Council for the Preservation of Anthropological Records (CoPAR) was originally founded to help "anthropologists, librarians, archivists, information specialists and

1 https://www.sfu.ca/ipinch/

others preserve and provide access to the record of human diversity and the history of the discipline", today "the preservation and stewardship of anthropological records face new challenges as anthropologists create records in many formats, both analog and digital, as expectations for immediate, digital access grow among users, and as collection managers face challenges of digitizing, preserving, and providing access to heterogeneous materials".[2] Entitled "Revitalizing CoPAR for the Digital Age", this community of engaged scholars is now working to help "create a roadmap for the preservation of anthropological research products in the digital age."

As we reflect on the challenges that lie ahead, Marshall McLuhan's penetrating insight that "in operational and practical fact, the medium is the message" (1964: 7) looks to have become both more and less true. The collapsing of time and space — epoch and distance — through online multimedia tools has generated widespread confusion about where content stops and where context begins. Should YouTube be understood as the publisher, host, owner or disseminator of digitized fragments of African cultural heritage, or does it play all (or none) of these roles? Can content be liberated from its container (a codec, a shell, a frame or a folder), or have form and content now been collapsed into one? Can digitized cultural heritage, once it has been uploaded to a shared public space, ever truly disappear or be retracted? Have new forms of digital media effected a transformative change on the durability and visibility of the messages that they transmit?

These timely questions have impacted all of our disciplines, including museum practice and curatorial studies. The development of critical museology as distinct from operational museology[3] is not only an "essential intellectual tool for better understanding museums, related exhibitionary institutions, fields of patrimony and counter patrimonies", but even more saliently:

> crucial for developing new exhibitionary genres, telling untold stories, rearticulating knowledge systems for public dissemination, reimagining organizational and management structures, and repurposing museums and galleries in line with multicultural and intercultural states and communities (Shelton 2013: 7).

---

2 http://archivescollaboratory.umd.edu/copar/

3 See Shelton (2013) for a helpful discussion.

Ever more museums of culture and ethnography are now engaged in complex and necessary conversations with the descendants of the people whose belongings (*not* objects), regalia (*not* costumes) and even ancestors (*not* human remains) they have the privilege and responsibility of ethically curating. Curatorial practice and archival practice are becoming more democratic and less authoritative. Curators of exhibits of cultural heritage regularly consult with communities for whom the collections have cultural meaning and relevance, sometimes leading to co-curation and even collaborative exhibit design.[4]

The title of this volume, *Searching for Sharing*, intentionally avoids the terminology of repatriation and return. In her introduction, Merolla introduced the concept of *reusability*, a term inherently more agnostic and more open to theoretical complexity. While the use of the prefix 're-' in words such as repatriate and return point to the undoing of some past action or deed (Glass 2004), the term *reuse* has a different directionality. After all, if the world's cultural heritage had not been "expatriated" to begin with — through colonization, imperial adventure and war — there would be less need for return and repatriation, let alone "rematriation" which has the more explicitly decolonial agenda of empowering women to collectively strengthen future generations through positive representation.[5]

The new pathways of digital publishing and dissemination — so powerfully embodied in Open Book Publishers and others who are productively rethinking the future of the academic book — are also working to unsettle established hierarchies of colonial authority, widen access to knowledge and thereby find innovative ways to coordinate medium with message in ways that McLuhan would surely have found provocative and welcome.

Searching for Sharing is the seventh volume in the World Oral Literature Series. The series was established to preserve and promote the oral literatures of indigenous communities by publishing materials on endangered traditions in ways that are both innovative and ethical. Situated at the intersection of anthropology and linguistics, the study

4 See Muntean *et al.* (2015).

5 https://newjourneys.ca/en/articles/we-are-the-rematriate-collective

of oral genres is an exciting and developing field, but one with few publishing outlets. The creative publishing practices adopted by Open Book Publishers make the dissemination of such unique traditions — in both textual and multimedia form — possible for the first time, recreating in the digital space some of the multimodal experience of the original recitation or performance that would otherwise be lost in traditional print.

As a case in point and to illustrate the transformative power of digital publishing, I am delighted to report that the updated and revised edition of Ruth Finnegan's masterpiece, *Oral Literature in Africa*, which Open Book republished in September 2012 and through which we launched the Oral Literature Series, has now been accessed, read online or downloaded over 116,000 times. Most importantly, the largest number of users per continent come from Africa, widening access to a readership that had been mostly excluded from the 1970 print edition. Similarly, although on a much more modest scale, *Oral Literature in the Digital Age: Archiving Orality and Connecting with Communities*, which I edited together with colleagues Claire Wheeler and Eleanor Wilkinson, has been viewed almost 12,000 times, with high numbers of readers from Asia — the focus of many of the chapters contained in its pages.

As Series Editor of the World Oral Literature Series, and the co-editor of this volume, I offer a few final words of thanks. A great deal of effort goes into creating the openness of such a volume, and the opportunities for sharing. We are extremely grateful to our colleague Jan Jansen who — with characteristic modesty and grace — oversaw much of the heavy lifting that brought this manuscript together, and then recused himself from taking credit as an editor. While his name does not grace the cover of this volume — at his own request, I hasten to add — his effort, diligence and generosity of spirit are present on every page. In *Searching for Sharing*, we also are fortunate to have published the work of a number of scholars for whom English is a third or even more distant language, and are thankful to our copy editor, Bridget Chase, who worked with these texts in a deliberate and respectful manner to support — through translation — the knowledge contained in these important voices. Much unremunerated labour goes into the production of such a volume, including the anonymous peer reviewers who donated their time and insights to improve the volume considerably, and the ever patient and professional staff at Open Book. I thank you all for your skill and commitment to this venture.

In conclusion, I hope that the readers of this volume have enjoyed these contributions as much as we enjoyed the process of collating them. We not only "searched for sharing" but also located it, together with a vibrant scholarly community, along the way. The journey was as important as the destination. The medium remains just as salient as the message.

References

Austin, J. L. (1962) *How to Do Things with Words: The William James Lectures, Delivered at Harvard University in 1955* (Oxford, Clarendon Press).

Glass, A. (2004) "Return to Sender: On the Politics of Cultural Property and the Proper Address of Art", *Journal of Material Culture* 9–2: 115–139.

McLuhan, M. (1964) *Understanding Media: The Extensions of Man* (New York, McGraw Hill).

Muntean, R., Hennessy, K., Antle, A., Rowley, S., Wilson, J. and Matkin, B. (2015) "ʔeləw̓kʷ — Belongings: Tangible Interactions with Intangible Heritage", *CITAR Journal* 7–2: 58–69.

Scott, M. K. (2012) "Engaging with Pasts in the Present: Curators, Communities, and Exhibition Practice", *Museum Anthropology* 35: 1–9.

Shelton, A. (2013) "Critical Museology: A Manifesto", *Museum Worlds: Advances in Research* 1: 7–23.

This book need not end here...

At Open Book Publishers, we are changing the nature of the traditional academic book. The title you have just read will not be left on a library shelf, but will be accessed online by hundreds of readers each month across the globe. OBP publishes only the best academic work: each title passes through a rigorous peer-review process. We make all our books free to read online so that students, researchers and members of the public who can't afford a printed edition will have access to the same ideas.
This book and additional content is available at:
https://www.openbookpublishers.com/product/590

Customize

Personalize your copy of this book or design new books using OBP and third-party material. Take chapters or whole books from our published list and make a special edition, a new anthology or an illuminating coursepack. Each customized edition will be produced as a paperback and a downloadable PDF. Find out more at:
https://www.openbookpublishers.com/section/59/1

Donate

If you enjoyed this book, and feel that research like this should be available to all readers, regardless of their income, please think about donating to us. We do not operate for profit and all donations, as with all other revenue we generate, will be used to finance new Open Access publications.
https://www.openbookpublishers.com/section/13/1/support-us

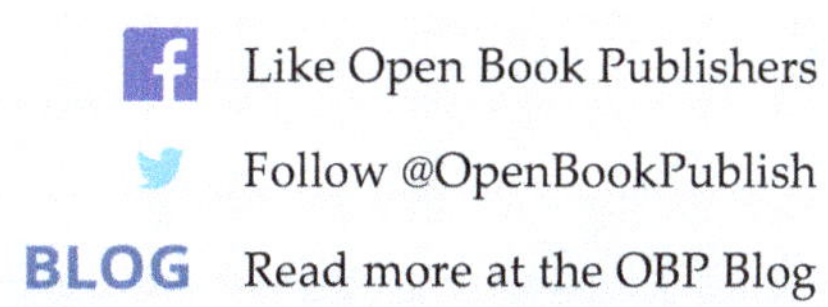

www.ingramcontent.com/pod-product-compliance
Lightning Source LLC
Chambersburg PA
CBHW061745270326
41928CB00011B/2377
* 9 7 8 1 7 8 3 7 4 3 1 8 6 *